Psychological Assessment
with the
Millon Clinical
Multiaxial Inventory (II):
An Interpretive Guide

Psychological Assessment with the Millon Clinical Multiaxial Inventory (II): An Interpretive Guide

by
Robert J. Craig, Ph.D., ABPP

PAR Psychological Assessment Resources,
P.O. Box 998/Odessa, Florida 33556

Library of Congress Cataloging-in-Publication Data

Craig, Robert, J.
  Psychological assessment with the Millon clinical multiaxial inventory: an interpretive guide / Robert J. Craig.
    p. cm.
  Includes bibliographical references.
  ISBN 0-911907-10-6
  1. Millon Clinical Multiaxial Inventory. 2. Personality disorders—Diagnosis. I. Title.
  [DNLM: 1. Personality Assessment. 2. Personality Inventory. 3. Personality
Disorders—diagnosis. 4. Psychiatric Status Rating Scales. WM 145 C886p 1993]
RC473.M47C73 1993
DNLM/DLC
for Library of Congress   93-11583
                                                      CIP

Printed in the United States of America   5 6 7 8 9   Reorder #RO-2434

TABLE OF CONTENTS

ROBERT J. CRAIG, PH.D.

PREFACE

The Millon Clinical Multiaxial Inventory (MCMI/MCMI-II) has become a popular clinical instrument and is being used increasingly in research. It consists of 22 scales that assess both personality styles/disorders and clinical symptoms or syndromes. Millon theorizes that clinical syndromes are simply extensions of basic personality styles, and he has developed a typology of personality pathology based on a theoretical model for the derivation of these basic styles. Millon's theory is summarized in Chapter 1. For more detailed information on this theory, the reader is referred to several works by Theodore Millon that are referenced at the end of Chapters 1 and 4.

Despite the more widespread use of this instrument, several reviews have bemoaned the "mysteries of interpretation" of this test. To date, there are two basic ways in which this test may be interpreted. First, examiners may hand score or computer score (through the National Computer Systems scoring services) the basic scales and then use their individual skills to formulate a personality description and suggested diagnosis. Second, and more commonly, the profile may be computer scored and a computer narrative report generated, which provides clinicians with a ready-made interpretation for the profile. However, many clinicians find the cost of this approach quite prohibitive, particularly for low-volume operations.

Another approach, and one that is more economical, is to develop a personality interpretive "cookbook," which provides clinicians with recommended or suggestive interpretations for scale scores and pattern configurations. This has been extensively done for other objective tests of personality, particularly with the *Minnesota Multiphasic Personality Inventory (MMPI/MMPI-2)*, the *16 Personality Factors (16PF)*, and the *California Psychological Inventory (CPI/CPI-R)*. Surprisingly, this has not been done to date for the MCMI-II. This present interpretive guide is an attempt to provide clinicians with an alternative approach to personality assessment using the MCMI-II, which has a rich history and is frequently used with other prominent personality instruments.

Personality interpretive "cookbook" manuals may be developed using several different methodologies. Many clinicians, particularly those inclined in the clinical/experimental direction, would opt for an actuarial approach to personality description. In this method, test profiles are compared with other data sets with the same patients until commonalities are empirically determined from common code types. This is rarely done, due to the costs and often longitudinal nature of the research design.

Another approach is to review the literature and abstract from individual research reports those characteristics or traits associated with certain profile codes. The "cookbook" author then writes a narrative description based on his or her interpretation of the profile code and incorporates whatever empirical results that pertain to the code into the description itself. This has been the general method used for the published MMPI, 16PF, and CPI interpretive manuals.

The MCMI is slightly different from other objective personality tests in that Millon used both a rational and a theoretical approach in constructing the test items and in validating the scales. Dr. Millon developed items based on his conception of the traits, behaviors, and symptoms seen in each of the personality disorders. The difference is that item selection was theory driven. Accordingly, when the clinician receives an MCMI (MCMI-II) computer-narrative report, it consists of the personality description, emanating from Millon's theory, of how the patient *should* behave, given the presence of certain characteristics.

This interpretive manual follows the same logic. Most of the descriptions are based on how the patient should behave, given the use of the MCMI/MCMI-II test and use of Millon's theory to describe the person. Presently there is very little substantive research to validate these descriptions. However, research on the MCMI/MCMI-II is beginning to appear in the professional literature with increasing frequency. A literature review by this author revealed that, through June, 1992, there were slightly over 300 published papers on the MCMI/MCMI-II. Papers about this test are now appearing at a rate of about 40-50 per year. This volume of research, though methodologically imperfect for experimental purists, can provide clinicians with guideposts and warning signals that will be helpful when using this test.

In order to prepare a document that would be useful for clinicians and heuristic to researchers, I first reviewed the entire published literature on the MCMI/MCMI-II, abstracting salient clinical findings that would be pertinent to MCMI-based personality descriptions. These were catalogued into various profile codes. Second, with the kind permission of Dr. Jim Choca, I abstracted from his recently published book on the MCMI (1992) selected "attenuated" (i.e., less pathologically based) personality descriptions and included them, where possible, in the established profile codes. Third, personality descriptions were composed based on my understanding of the constructs measured by the scales, but in accordance with Millon's biopsychosocial theory of personality pathology. Finally, any research that would be clinically relevant was added for information purposes. The references that pertain to these citations are included at the end of Chapter 4. The reader should keep in mind, however, that these interpretations are largely based on Millon's theory, which was the basis for the development of the scales, and from my clinical experience and that of a number of authors who provided profile interpretations in published journals. There is very little published data on the validity of these interpretations, and the reader should consider them as interpretive hypotheses to explore with clients in a professional relationship.

This manual is divided into five chapters. The first chapter presents Millon's theory, the development and description of the test, and an explanation of how to use this interpretive guide. Chapters 2 through 4 present suggested interpretations of single scale elevations (i.e., one-point codes) for the 22 MCMI-II personality and clinical syndrome scales, including the validity indices, and suggested interpretations for the MCMI-II configural codes (i.e., two-point, three-point, four-point, and high-ranging codes). Some codes provide only brief descriptions of personality; clinicians are encouraged to consult Chapter 2 for more elaborate descriptions of the scale interpretations in order to develop a more elegant personality interpretation than the one briefly synopsized in the configuration. Chapter 5 presents several case examples to illustrate how the MCMI-II may be integrated into an objective test battery.

Readers of this manual assume the ultimate responsibility for its use. Final evaluation, personality description, and diagnosis must rest on decisions based on multiple sources of information. The interpretive guide only provides useful areas for further inquiry by the clinician and researcher. Also, the MCMI was normed on clinical populations and was not meant to be used in nonclinical settings. Use of this test and this guide with persons who are not being assessed or treated in clinical settings is not appropriate.

1. INTRODUCTION

This chapter briefly describes the development of the MCMI and MCMI-II, discusses its psychometric properties, explains the concept of Base Rate (BR) scores upon which code types are based, and then illustrates the use of this interpretive guide.

CLINICAL PERSONOLOGY

Millon argues that the ideal structure of clinical science, referred to as "personology," contains the components of *theory, taxonomy, instrumentation,* and *intervention.* Theory provides a conceptual basis to explain the observed phenomenon. Taxonomy provides a method, preferably theory driven, to classify the phenomenon. Instrumentation is a set of tools that assess the constructs of the theory, and intervention refers to the techniques and strategies commonly known as therapy.

Although Millon has become identified with instrumentation, particularly with the MCMI-II, he is first and foremost a theorist, and his instrumentation derives from his theory of personality and personality pathology, termed a biopsychosocial theory. In order to fully understand the MCMI-II, it is necessary to first understand Millon's theory.

BIOPSYCHOSOCIAL THEORY OF PERSONALITY AND PERSONALITY PATHOLOGY

Millon's (1990) theory defines three personologic polarities: *survival aims, adaptive modes,* and *replication strategies.* He argues that the first task of existence is to survive. Goals for survival may range from merely existing to enhancing and actualizing our existence. Behaviors that threaten our existence are organized on a *pain* polarity, while behaviors that enhance the meaning of life are organized on a *pleasure* polarity.

Next, individuals adapt to their environment; they may do so either by *actively* trying to change their environment or by *passively* allowing the environment to change them.

Finally, in using replication strategies, individuals may either focus on themselves *(self-centered)* or engage in nurturing behaviors *(other-centered).*

How we seek reinforcement (active, passive)—an adaptive mode—and the *source* of reinforcement (independent, dependent, ambivalent, discordant, detached)—a replication strategy—provides the essential taxonomy of the theory. When the two basic modes of adaptation are combined with the five sources of reinforcement, 10 basic personality patterns are derived from theory. Table 1.1 presents the initial classification schema for the 10 basic personality styles.

Table 1.1
Millon's Basic Personality Styles

	Independent (self)	Dependent (others)	Ambivalent (conflicted)	Discordant (reversal)	Detached (none)
Active	Unruly	Sociable	Sensitive	Forceful	Inhibited
Passive	Confident	Cooperative	Respectful	Defeatist	Introversive

These are theoretical types, and no one person would be expected to demonstrate a pure pattern. Normally, the individual's personality represents a combination of two or more of these basic patterns.

Each pattern or style can range from normal to dysfunctional, and the latter can range from mild to severely disturbed. Millon believes that personality pathology is merely an exaggeration of the individual's basic personality style. The resulting personality pathology, called personality disorder, results from a complex interaction of biological dispositions, maladaptive learning, and environmental stresses. The theory posits 10 personality disorders and three severe dysfunctional variants based on the five sources of reinforcement and the two modes of adaptation. The resulting matrix of personality disorder pathology is presented in Table 1.2.

Millon defines personality pathology as a deficiency in the capacity to balance the three personologic polarities (survival, adaptation, replication). Each personality disorder is provided with clinical domain criteria in order to systematically study the structural and functional characteristics within the behavioral (expressive acts, interpersonal conduct), phenomenological (cognitive style, objective representations, self-image), intrapsychic (regulatory mechanisms, morphological organization), and biophysical (mood/temperament) domains. For a more detailed explanation of this theory, the reader should consult one or more of the many excellent references on this topic (McMahon, 1992; Millon 1981, 1984a, 1984b, 1986a, 1986b, 1986c, 1990; Millon & Everly, 1985).

Table 1.2
Millon's Framework for Personality Pathology

Pathology Domain	Self – Other			Pain – Pleasure	
Source of Reinforcement	Other + Self –	Self + Other	Self <-> Other	Pain – Pleasure	Pleasure – Pain ±
Coping Style	Dependent	Independent	Ambivalent	Discordant	Detached
Passive Variant	Dependent	Narcissistic	Compulsive	Self-Defeating (Masochistic)	Schizoid
Active Variant	Histrionic	Antisocial	Passive – Aggressive	Aggressive (sadistic)	Avoidant
Dysfunctional Variant	Borderline	Paranoid		Borderline or Paranoid	Schizotypal

Note. From *Millon Clinical Multiaxial Inventory-II: Manual for the MCMI-II* (2nd ed.) (p. 19) by T. Millon, 1987, Minneapolis: National Computer Systems. Copyright 1977, 1982, 1983, 1987 by Theodore Millon. Adapted by permission.

Once the theory has evolved and a taxonomy has been established, the next step is to develop instrumentation to measure the theory-derived disorders.

CONSTRUCTION OF THE MCMI AND MCMI-II

State-of-the-art validation processes require that validation be an integral part of each phase of test development. The MCMI and MCMI-II were developed according to a three-stage process. In the *theoretical-substantive* phase, items were written and then evaluated according to how well their content corresponded with theory. For example, the Antisocial Personality Disorder represents the Active Independent personality style, according to theory. Rather than relying on items that pertain to antisocial acts, which are often used to define the disorder, Millon chose to develop items that pertained to his conceptualization of the Antisocial personality style (representing an active and independent personality style). Thus, a representative item from this scale, keyed "true," is "There are members of my family who say I'm selfish and think only of myself."

Millon (1985, 1986a) believes that it is not necessary to tap all the defining characteristics of a disorder in order to accurately assess it. In fact, none of the items on any MCMI-II scale reflect every domain of the disorder. Only representative items have been selected, with the understanding that endorsement of items that define essential elements of the disorder will accurately assess the disorder itself.

During this phase, the initial pool of face-valid items was created. Some items were eliminated due to problems with readability, patient judgment regarding the ease of self-rating, and expert clinicians' blind sorting of the items into theory-relevant categories. The remaining 1100-item pool was split into two equivalent forms.

In the *internal-structural* phase, the test items were evaluated according to how well they interrelated and fit Millon's overall model of psychopathology. For example, the item mentioned above as representative of the Antisocial personality scale is also included on the Narcissistic scale because it reflects the egocentric self-image of the narcissist. It remains keyed on the Antisocial Personality Disorder scale because empirical research and clinical observation have confirmed that many patients with an Antisocial Personality Disorder also have a Narcissistic personality style.

During this phase, the two equivalent forms were administered to clinical samples, and items were retained that had the highest item-total scale correlation. Item-scale intercorrelations and item endorsement frequencies were calculated, and items with extreme endorsement frequencies (<.15 and >.85) were eliminated because of their poor discriminative efficiency. The remaining 440 items were eventually reduced to 289.

The final step in the validation process was the *external-criterion* phase, in which each test scale was evaluated to determine the degree of correspondence with other measures of the disorder or syndrome. In this phase, 167 clinicians administered the test to a total of 682 patients and completed a uniform diagnostic instruction booklet that gave clinical descriptions of each theory-based personality prototype and clinical syndrome. Twenty criterion groups were formed that corresponded to each of the MCMI scale disorders/syndromes. The test was then reduced to 150 items, three scales were eliminated (Hypochondrias, Obsession-Compulsion, and Sociopathy), and three scales were added (Hypomania, Alcohol Abuse, and Drug Abuse). The construction steps were repeated, and this resulted in a 175-item self-report inventory, published as the Millon Clinical Multiaxial Inventory (Millon, 1983).

Millon sees validation as an ongoing process. With evolutions in theory, revisions in psychiatric nomenclature, and empirical research identifying certain problems with the instrument (particularly the excessive item overlap), the MCMI was revised, again according to the model described above. A provisional form of the MCMI-II was developed with 368 items. Sadistic and Self-Defeating scales were added. The Antisocial scale was subdivided into Antisocial and Aggressive (Sadistic), and the Passive-Aggressive scale was subdivided into Passive-Aggressive and Self-Defeating (Masochistic). Three modifier (validity) scales were added (Disclosure, Desirability, Debasement). A total of 45 items were changed, and an item-weighting system (1-3) was developed that assigned weights to scored responses, with the prototype items for each scale given the highest weight (3). Also, some scales were renamed. Table 1.3 presents the scale designations for the MCMI and the MCMI-II. In the criterion-validation phase of the revision, a provisional form of the MCMI-II was administered to 184 patients and the validation process continued as previously described (Millon, 1987). A total of 1292 patients (643 males, 649 females) composed the MCMI-II normative sample.

Comparisons between the MCMI and MCMI-II scale designations appear in Table 1.3. The first 10 scales of the MCMI-II (Scales 1 - 8B) assess basic personality styles/disorders, and the next three scales (S, C, and P) assess the more severe and pathological personality disorders. The next six scales (A, H, N, D, B, and T) assess the less severe clinical syndromes, and the last three scales (SS, CC, and PP) measure the more severe symptom disorders.

Table 1.3
MCMI-I and MCMI-II Scale Designations

MCMI-I Scales	MCMI-II Scales
Basic Personality Patterns	**Clinical Personality Patterns**
1. Schizoid (Asocial)	1. Schizoid
2. Avoidant	2. Avoidant
3. Dependent (Submissive)	3. Dependent
4. Histrionic (Gregarious)	4. Histrionic
5. Narcissistic	5. Narcissistic
6. Antisocial (Aggressive)	6A. Antisocial
	6B. Aggressive
7. Compulsive (Conforming)	7. Compulsive
8. Passive-Aggressive (Negative)	8A. Passive-Aggressive
	8B. Self-Defeating
Pathological Personality Disorders	**Severe Personality Pathology**
S Schizotypal	S Schizotypal
C Borderline (Cycloid)	C Borderline
P Paranoid	P Paranoid
Clinical Syndromes	**Clinical Syndromes**
A Anxiety	A Anxiety
H Somatoform	H Somatoform Disorder
N Hypomania	N Bipolar: Manic Disorder
D Dysthymia	D Dysthymic Disorder
B Alcohol Abuse	B Alcohol Dependence
T Drug Abuse	T Drug Dependence
SS Thought Disorder	
CC Psychotic Depression	**Severe Syndromes**
PP Delusional Disorder	SS Thought Disorder
	CC Major Depression
	PP Delusional Disorder
	Modifier Indices
	X Disclosure
	Y Desirability
	Z Debasement

BASE RATE SCORES

In 1955, Meehl and Rosen published a paper arguing that the diagnostic accuracy of personality tests could be improved when base rates or prevalence data are taken into account. Until the publication of the MCMI, no test in psychology used this concept to establish a diagnosis. Most use some type of raw score transformation to normalize the distribution in order to provide comparable frequency spreads. However, personality disorders and clinical syndromes are not normally distributed. In these cases, it would be more desirable to convert raw scores based on the rate the disorder occurs in a population. The MCMI and MCMI-II convert raw scores into Base Rate (BR) scores. Millon (1983) defines a BR score as a transformed score "determined by known personality and syndrome data and by using cutting lines designed to maximize correct diagnostic classification" (p. 10).

The BR conversion scores were developed based on prevalence data of Axis I disorders among 713 clinical patients in treatment and prevalence data of Axis II disorders among a representative national group of 937 patients with the disorder. The raw score distribution was reviewed, and the point on the scale above which the percentage of scores was equal to the base rate of occurrence within the population studied was determined. An ordinal value—the BR score—was arbitrarily assigned to this distribution. A BR score of 20 is equal to the 10th percentile for the clinical standardization sample, a BR of 40 is equal to the 20th percentile, and a BR of 60 is at the median. A BR score of 75-84 suggests the syndrome or disorder is present, while a BR score of >84 suggests the syndrome is prominent. This is the point at which higher scores are equal to the prevalence base rate for the personality pattern or clinical syndrome clinically judged most prominent and which optimizes the diagnostic classification ratio of valid-to-false positives for those assessments. In other words, a BR>84 indicates that the individual has all the characteristics defined by the disorder or syndrome (Hsu & Maruish, 1992).

For the MCMI-I, BR scores were derived from test scores from 1591 patients from over 100 hospitals and outpatient clinics and from almost 40 private practices in 27 states and Great Britain. A cross-validation sample of 256 patients was also utilized. For the MCMI-II, BR scores were derived from studies using a randomly selected group of 519 clinicians, who administered both the MCMI-I and the MCMI-II to between one and three patients, and who also completed Axis I and II diagnostic information on these patients. This study contributed 825 cases to the normative population. The second study used 93 experienced MCMI test users, who contributed an additional 467 cases. These samples were then combined to form the normative group (N=1292). Over 80% were from outpatient settings.

Because the MCMI-II has championed the use of base rates and base rate scores, clinical researchers are beginning to compare the diagnostic utility of personality instruments, particularly the MCMI-II, with different populations (Baldessarini, Findlestein, & Arana, 1983; Gibertini, 1992; Gibertini, Brandenberg, & Retzlaff, 1986). This type of research is encouraging and brings a more scientific approach to the study of clinical personology.

RESPONSE STYLE INDICES AND ADJUSTMENTS

The MCMI-II contains four validity scales and two adjustment corrections.

Validity Index. This consists of four items, each having an endorsement frequency of <.01. These items are of such an improbable nature (e.g., "There never has been any hair on my head or my body.") that, if they are endorsed as "true," it may suggest random responding, confusion, or carelessness. Millon finds this preferable to the many contorted ways of assessing profile validity that have been established for the MMPI.

Disclosure Index. This assesses whether the patient is providing sufficient information on the test for reliable diagnosis. It functions similarly to the K scale of the MMPI. A high disclosure level results in a scoring procedure that reduces the BR scores on all scales; a low disclosure level increases scores on all scales.

Desirability Gauge. This assesses "faked-good" tendencies, or presenting oneself in a highly favorable manner. The median BR score for patients who were judged to show this response style was 81, and the median BR for persons simulating a faked-good approach was 96. An elevated score on the Desirability Gauge results in a scoring correction that increases BR scores on the scales of Schizotypal, Borderline, Anxiety, Somatoform, and Dysthymia.

Debasement Measure. This determines the extent to which patients are presenting themselves in an unfavorable light, emphasizing their psychopathology. The median BR score for patients on this gauge was 87, while persons who were asked to simulate a faked-bad response style attained a median BR score of 108. A low score on Debasement decreases scores on the scales of Schizotypal, Borderline, Anxiety, Somatoform, and Dysthymia.

The above validity scale indices appear on the MCMI-II profile sheet. The next two adjustment measures do not directly appear on the profile, but are used to make adjustments on certain scales based on test-taking attitudes and clinical conditions.

Denial vs. Complaint Adjustment. This procedure makes adjustments for patients who deny or emphasize their psychological pain. Elevated scores on Histrionic, Compulsive, and Narcissistic result in a correction that raises patients' scores on Schizotypal, Borderline, Paranoid, Anxiety, and Dysthymia; elevated scores on Avoidant and Self-Defeating lowers scores on these same scales.

High Depression/Anxiety Adjustment. This correction makes adjustments for those in acute emotional turmoil, based on scores on Anxiety and Dysthymia. Adjustments decrease scores on Avoidant, Self-Defeating, and

Borderline. Also, a recent inpatient admission, the presence of an Axis I syndrome, or a clinical episode whose duration is less than 1 week and/or 1 to 4 weeks results in a correction that increases scores on Thought Disorder, Delusional Disorder, and Major Depression.

In general, the test should be considered invalid if (a) 12 or more items have been omitted, (b) two or more items on the Validity Index have been marked "True," (c) Scale X scores are <144 or >591, or (d) the BR scores on all basic personality scales are <60.

PSYCHOMETRIC FEATURES

The *reliability* and *validity* of the MCMI and MCMI-II have been studied extensively with different clinical populations. This work is presented in detail in the major source books on the MCMI-II; the reader is urged to consult these references for a more in-depth analysis (Choca, Shanley, & VanDenberg, 1992; Craig, 1993). In general, consistent with theory, the stability coefficients for the personality scales are higher than those for the clinical syndrome scales. Both are adequate for measurement purposes. The validity of the test has been assessed by correlating the MCMI-II scales with scales from similar instruments, comparing computer-generated diagnosis with that assigned by a clinician, studying the test's classification accuracy (positive predictive power, negative predictive power) compared to other instruments, and using discriminant function analysis and factor analytic studies for convergence with theory.

PROFILE INTERPRETATION

Following is a model for the interpretation of the MCMI-II:

1. Evaluate patient background information (demographic data, mental status, clinical interview material, other test results, known stresses, etc.).

2. Appraise the response style using scales X, Y, and Z and the Validity Index.

3. Assess the basic personality style using the personality disorder scales.

4. Assess for the presence of clinical syndromes using the clinical syndrome scales.

5. Determine the severity of the disorder(s) and syndrome(s).

6. Check for particular critical test items of clinical importance (e.g., "Serious thoughts of suicide have occurred to me for many years.").

7. Establish a diagnosis.

8. Write a personality description based on these assessments. Attempt to understand the meaning of the clinical syndrome(s) for the patient's personality functioning.

9. Determine treatment implications and recommendations.

Using This Interpretive Guide

The coding of the profiles in this guide follows a common pattern. All numbers and letters correspond to the scale designations in the MCMI-II test manual for that scale. The first number in the code represents the personality scale with the highest score, followed by the second highest and then third highest, when applicable. In some cases, the clinical scales were among the highest scores in the code. In these cases, the few highest personality scales were given initial prominence in the code, followed by the clinical syndrome scale(s). In order to appear in the code, a scale must have had a BR score >74, unless otherwise specified in the code descriptions.

First, each profile code begins with a suggested interpretation for the profile. Second, a suggested diagnosis is presented. Third, subclinical (nonpathological) personality descriptors may be given for use in nonclinical cases (research only). Fourth, salient clinical research that pertains to the code is briefly summarized.

Some profile code descriptions have all of this information available, while others have only some of this information included in the description. These cases indicate that there is little information in the literature upon which to base the presentation of the material other than a personality description that emanates from theory.

If clinicians encounter an MCMI-II test protocol for which a code type is not available, an interpretation may be developed by consulting the sections on individual scale interpretation in Chapter 2 and combining the highest two or three personality scale interpretations into the description.

References: Chapter 1

Baldessarini, R. J., Findlestein, S., & Arana, G. W. (1983). The predictive power of diagnostic tests and the effect of prevalence of illness. *Archives of General Psychiatry, 40,* 569-573.

Choca, J. P., Shanley, L. A., & VanDenberg, E. (1992). *Interpretive guide to the Millon Clinical Multiaxial Inventory.* Washington, DC: American Psychological Association.

Craig, R. J. (Ed.) (1993). *Millon Clinical Multiaxial Inventory: A clinical research information synthesis.* Hillsdale, NJ: Lawrence Erlbaum.

Gibertini, M. (1992). Factors affecting the operating characteristics of the MCMI-II. In R. Craig (Ed.), *Millon Clinical Multiaxial Inventory: A clinical research information synthesis* (pp. 71-80). Hillsdale, NJ: Lawrence Erlbaum.

Gibertini, M., Brandenburg, N. A., & Retzlaff, P. D. (1986). The operating characteristics of the Millon Clinical Multiaxial Inventory. *Journal of Personality Assessment, 50,* 554-567.

Hsu, L. M., & Maruish, M. E. (1992). *Conducting publishable research with the MCMI-II: Psychometric and statistical issues.* Minneapolis: National Computer Systems.

McMahon, R. C. (1992). The Millon Clinical Multiaxial Inventory: An introduction to theory, development, and interpretation. In R. Craig (Ed.), *Millon Clinical Multiaxial Inventory: A clinical research information synthesis* (pp. 3-22). Hillsdale, NJ: Lawrence Erlbaum.

Meehl, P. E., & Rosen, A. (1955). Antecendent probability and the efficiency of psychometric signs, patterns, or cutting scores. *Psychological Bulletin, 52,* 194-216.

Millon, T. (1981). *Disorders of personality: DSM-III: Axis II.* New York: Wiley.

Millon, T. (1983). *Millon Clinical Multiaxial Inventory Manual* (3rd ed.). Minneapolis: National Computer Systems.

Millon, T. (1984a). On the renaissance of personality assessment and personality theory. *Journal of Personality Assessment, 48,* 450-466.

Millon, T. (1984b). Interpretive guide to the Millon Clinical Multiaxial Inventory. In P. McReynolds & G. J. Chelune (Eds.), *Advances in personality assessment: Vol. 6* (pp. 1-41). San Francisco: Jossey-Bass.

Millon, T. (1985). The MCMI provides a good assessment of DSM-III disorders: The MCMI-II will prove even better. *Journal of Personality Assessment, 49,* 379-391.

Millon, T. (1986a). The MCMI and DSM-III: Further commentaries. *Journal of Personality Assessment, 50,* 205-207.

Millon, T. (1986b). A theoretical derivation of pathological personalities. In T. Millon & G. Klerman (Eds.), *Contemporary directions in psychopathology: Toward the DSM-IV* (pp. 639-669). New York: Guilford.

Millon, T. (1986c). Personality prototypes and their diagnostic criteria. In T. Millon & G. Klerman (Eds.), *Contemporary directions in psychopathology: Toward the DSM-IV* (pp. 671-712). New York: Guilford.

Millon, T. (1987). *Millon Clinical Multiaxial Inventory-II: Manual for the MCMI-II.* Minneapolis: National Computer Systems.

Millon, T. (1990). *Toward a new personology: An evolutional model.* New York: Wiley-Interscience.

Millon, T., & Everly, G. (1985). *Personality and its disorders: A biosocial learning approach.* New York: Wiley.

2. MODIFIER AND CORRECTION INDICES

Built into the MCMI-II are several items designed to measure the validity of the profile by screening out individuals who are unable or unwilling to answer openly and appropriately or who try to present themselves either more favorably or less favorably than indicated upon objective review. This chapter briefly describes the four correction indices and presents validity configurations which may be used to judge these tendencies.

VALIDITY INDEX

This index consists of four highly unusual items endorsed "true." It is sensitive to poor reading ability, careless or random responding, and confused emotional states.

- If the index (raw score) is 0, then profile is valid and interpretable.
- If the raw score is 1, then caution is recommended in interpreting the profile.
- An R of 2 or more suggests that the profile is probably invalid and should not be interpreted. Also, if 12 or more items are unanswered, the profile should not be interpreted.

DISCLOSURE LEVEL (SCALE X)

This scale reflects whether or not the patient was open and cooperative with the testing process by appropriately disclosing, or was reticent and secretive in responding to the items. It is calculated by the degree of positive or negative deviation from the mid-range of an adjusted composite raw score of 10 basic personality scales. Equation-driven corrections are made only if the adjusted raw score is greater than 400 or less than 250. If the sum is less than 145 or greater than 590, the profile is invalid and should not be interpreted.

A low score on Scale X suggests

- defensiveness and a purposeful unwillingness to report symptoms, feelings, and problems
- personality traits that include hesitancy and reserve, and a need for social approval that requires the avoidance of criticism
- a general naiveté about psychological matters, including a lack of self-insight and introspection

Low scores on this scale also suggest problems in entering into a treatment alliance and a probable uncooperative attitude and response toward psychotherapeutic interventions. Answering "false" to a majority of items will produce a low score on this index. A high score suggests an unusually open and self-revealing attitude toward discussing one's emotional difficulties.

DESIRABILITY GAUGE (SCALE Y)

This scale reflects the tendency to place oneself in a favorable light. Patients who score in elevated ranges on Scale Y

- are presenting themselves as morally virtuous, emotionally balanced, and composed with few or no psychological problems

- are presenting an image of confidence and gregariousness

- tend to be organized, efficient, and moralistic in the sense of respecting authority and following societal rules

Extremely high scores may be problematic in that the patient may be actually concealing psychological, symptomatic, or interpersonal difficulties.

DEBASEMENT MEASURE (SCALE Z)

This scale reflects tendencies opposite to those of Scale Y. On occasion both indexes are high, especially among patients who are unusually self-disclosing (Scale X).

High scores suggest a tendency to depreciate or devalue oneself by presenting emotional and personal difficulties in stronger terms that are likely to be uncovered upon objective review (e.g., symptom exaggeration).

Patients with high scores

- are reporting that they feel empty
- have low self-esteem
- become angry or tearful easily
- feel tense, guilty, and depressed, and possibly engage in self-destructive behaviors

Especially high scores (BR>85) may reflect a cry for help and feelings of acute distress. Here, the patient believes he or she is experiencing an especially distressing level of emotional turmoil, or may be responding to the items in such a way as to call our attention to his or her situation.

Validity Configurations

1. Low scores on X and Y with a high score on Z suggests a moderate exaggeration of current emotional problems.

2. High scores on Y and low scores on scales X and Z (an "arrow" configuration pointing right) suggests a response set emphasizing looking psychologically healthy.

3. A low score on Y and high scores on X and Z (an "arrow" configuration pointing left) suggests a response set emphasizing looking psychologically maladjusted.

4. High scores on Y (BR>80) and a low score on Z (BR<30) suggests a possibly faking good response set.

5. High scores on Z (BR>85) and low scores on Y (BR<40) suggests symptom and problem exaggeration.

Note. Millon (1987) reported, and research has confirmed, that the MCMI is better able to detect faked-bad than faked-good profiles. This suggests that caution should be exercised in using the MCMI in clinical situations where clients are motivated to deny problems.

Research

1. The Validity Index was able to detect up to 98% of profiles from college students who responded to the test in a random manner (Bagby, Gillis, & Rogers, 1991). However, 2% of patients with sexual perversions would have been excluded as "faking" by the index (Langevin, Lang, Reynolds, Wright, Garrels, Marchese, Handy, Pugh, & Frenzel, 1988).

2. Retzlaff, Sheehan, and Fiel (1991) found that Scale X was a poor predictor of faked-good profiles but very good at detecting faked-bad profiles. Scale X was only moderately effective in detecting malingering.

3. Wetzler and Marlowe (1990) reported that Scale Z of a BR>84 would have excluded 17% of patients as "faking bad" when they in fact had psychopathology.

4. Patients feigning Post-Traumatic Syndrome scored BR<60 on Scales X and Z (Lees-Haley, 1992).

References for Chapters 2-4 appear at the end of Chapter 4.

3. ONE-POINT CODES

This chapter presents suggested interpretations for Millon's 10 basic personality disorder scales plus three severe dysfunctional variants. This is followed by descriptions of the nine clinical syndrome scales. The heading for each scale is supplemented by a one-word descriptor for the subclinical type (in parentheses) and a phrase describing the basic personality style that underlies the disorder, according to Millon's theory. These descriptions have been constructed on the basis of my clinical experience and that of other clinicians published in the available literature, guided by Millon's theory of personality pathology. The factors included in each interpretation are drawn from behavioral, phenomenological, intrapsychic, and biophysical domains. Each description is followed by the DSM-III-R diagnosis and relevant research, if available.

PERSONALITY DISORDER SCALES

Schizoid (1) (asocial) *Passive Detached Type*

High scorers display deficits primarily in emotional, interpersonal, social, and behavioral aspects of personality.

These people appear apathetic, dull, quiet, colorless, vague, aloof, and introverted. They seem lost in their surroundings, blending into the background, or engaging in vague pursuits. They show limited enthusiasm for most activities, preferring a solitary life, and rarely initiate conversation. They seem indifferent to social relationships and do not seek social contact. They seem to have a low need for social involvement. They seem to require little affection, and lack both warmth and emotional expression. They manifest an emotionally bland appearance with flattened affect, combined with a lack of sensitivity to their own feelings and those of others. They lack an outward expression of aggression. They often are asexual, perhaps due to their relationship deficits. They are quite content to be passive, detached, and distant in their relationships and have few friends, preferring the life of a loner. The detachment is not a defense mechanism. They are comfortable this way and prefer it, at least at the conscious level. Underneath this detachment lies a rich fantasy life and excessive daydreaming. Intrapsychically they are in a chronic dilemma, because they cannot be in a relationship without fearing engulfment, nor can they be without a relationship without feeling intense aloneness. If married or in a committed relationship, problems are likely to arise with spousal complaints of a lack of involvement and intimacy. Others see them as strange and "spacey." Relationship deficits are likely to be serious. These people have a low self-esteem, but more often have difficulty expressing how they feel about themselves. Their thinking can be obscure at times with cognitive slippage occasionally manifested in speech. Their thoughts are vague and unfocused. Depersonalization, feelings of emptiness, and identity diffusion are also part of their personality structure. These patients tend to drift through marginal aspects of society. When social demands become inescapable they are prone to anxiety reactions, somatoform disorders, and brief reactive psychoses.

Diagnosis. Schizoid Personality Disorder.

Subclinical. Solitary, reserved, and distant.

Avoidant (2) *Active Detached Type*

High-scoring patients manifest deficits primarily in the social and interpersonal areas of personality.

These patients present as socially awkward, withdrawn, introverted, and self-conscious. Because they are hypersensitive to rejection and fear negative evaluations, they either try to maintain a good social appearance despite their underlying fear, or they withdraw from social contacts. Tension, anxiety, and anger may also be present, but all stemming from the same issue—a desire for social acceptance and their fear of rejection. Most often they maintain a social distance in order to avoid any further experience of being rejected. They are devastated by perceived signs of disapproval and tend to withdraw, thus reducing the chance to enhance relationships. This results in social isolation despite a very strong need for social relatedness. These patients can put on a pleasant appearance to mask their underlying social anxiety, but they have a pervasive belief that others will be disparaging of them. Their essential conflict is a strong desire to relate but an equally strong expectation of disapproval, depreciation, and rejection. This results in keeping others at a distance but also in loneliness, isolation, and continued shyness and timidity. They are at risk for social phobias.

Diagnosis. Avoidant Personality Disorder.

Subclinical. Shy, lonely, insecure, sensitive to rejection.

Dependent (3) (submissive-dependent) *Passive Dependent Type*

High scorers show personality deficits primarily in the social and interpersonal spheres.

These patients tend to lean on other people for security, support, guidance, and direction. They are passive, submissive, dependent, and self-conscious, and they lack initiative, confidence, and autonomy. Their temperament is pacifying and they try to avoid conflict. They acquiesce to maintain nurturance, affection, protection, and security. They can be expected to be obliging, docile, and placating while seeking relationships in which they can lean on others for emotional support. They have excessive needs for attachment and to be taken care of, and they feel helpless when alone. They willingly submit to the wishes of others in order to maintain this security. When threatened with a loss of this security, they seek out other relationships or institutions to take care of them. Their basic conflict is a fear of abandonment. This leads them to be overly compliant in order to ensure themselves of enduring protection. Their need for support is overwhelming. They prefer the dependent state and are genuinely docile. They have a self-image as a weak and fragile person, avoiding responsibilities and thereby precluding any chance of autonomy. When stressed (with a disruption of security), they are prone to develop anxiety and depressive disorders and substance abuse problems.

Note. Millon's theory argues that this style is not a veneer that masks deeply held resentments, a view held by traditional psychodynamic thinking, which posits that these people are quite angry and resentful toward those who provide them with the needed safety and security. The core motivation for the dependent personality is to obtain and maintain nurturance and supportive relationships. It is quite possible that a person can act both passively and assertively to accomplish this central goal.

It has been theorized that some form of overprotection during childhood development years produces this style, in that these patients were not given the opportunity to learn autonomous behaviors.

Diagnosis. Dependent Personality Disorder.

Subclinical. Passive, docile, trustful, naive.

Research.

1. This was the modal MCMI profile for a group of (*N*=23) head injury patients being evaluated for Worker's Compensation claims (Snibbe, Peterson, & Sosner, 1980).

2. Women who elected mastectomy, compared to women who elected more conservative treatment for breast cancer, scored higher on the Avoidant scale, suggesting they attempt to react to stress by attempting to avoid or escape it (actually or in fantasy) (Wolberg, Tanner, Romsaas, Trump, & Malec, 1987).

3. Donat, Geczy, Helmrich, and LeMay (1992) found this code among 66/195 (34%) of psychiatric inpatients.

4. This was the modal profile for female bulimics (*N*=37), reflecting passivity, conflict avoidance, eagerness to please, self-sacrificing behaviors, poor self-image, and a Pollyannaish cognitive style (Tisdale, Pendleton, & Marlow, 1990).

Histrionic (4) (gregarious) *Active Dependent Type*

High scorers show deficits primarily in social relationships.

Expect these patients to be overly dramatic, with strong needs to be the center of attention. They are seductive, through speech, style, dress, or manner, and seek constant stimulation and excitement in an exhibitionistic-like atmosphere requiring praise and attention. They are emotionally labile, easily excited, and evince frequent emotional outbursts. They are very gregarious, assertive, and socially outgoing, but manipulate people to draw their approval and affection. They have strong needs for constant social acceptance so they are socially facile and seductively engaging, such that others are drawn to their gregarious and enchanting manner. Relationships are often shallow and strained, however, due to their repeated dramatic and emotional outbursts and their self-centeredness. Denial and repression are their main defenses. Millon's theory posits that these patients are motivated by power strivings. They court the favor of others, but beneath the persona of confidence and self-assurance is a fear of autonomy and independence that requires a constant need for acceptance and approval. They tend to displace anxieties when stressed. They are at risk for somatoform disorders and marital problems.

Narcissistic (5) *Passive Independent Type*

High scorers show deficits primarily in their sense of self. (This scale emphasizes the egocentric arrogance of the narcissist.)

These patients are quite self-centered; they expect people to recognize their special qualities, and they require constant praise and recognition. They have excessive expectations of entitlement and demand special favors. Grandiose statements of self-importance are readily elicited, and they consider themselves particularly attractive. They appear arrogant, haughty, conceited, boastful, snobbish, pretentious, and supercilious. They will exploit people and manipulate them with an air of superiority. Although they can be momentarily charming, they have a deficient social conscience and think only of themselves. They show a social imperturbability and are likely to disregard social constraints. They exploit social relationships, are indifferent to the rights of others, relate in an autocratic manner, and expect others to focus on them. Although this basic style often alienates other people, they respond with a sense of contempt and indifference, because their inflated sense of self needs no confirmation from other people. They are quite grandiose, arrogant, and are unlikely to show signs of self-doubt. If they are humiliated or experience a narcissistic injury, they are prone to develop an affective disorder and perhaps paranoia. Many substance abusers also have a narcissistic personality style.

Diagnosis. Narcissistic Personality Disorder.

Subclinical. Positive self-image, self-centered, overconfident, cool, vain, charming, manipulative.

Research.

1. Antoni, Tischer, Levine, Green, and Millon (1985b) found that many patients with an MMPI 42/24 Code had an elevated Scale 5 on the MCMI.

2. Repko and Cooper (1985) found this code among a group of Worker's Compensation claimants with orthopedic complaints.

3. Antoni, Levine, Tischer, Green, and Millon (1986) found that many patients with an MMPI 89/98 Code had an elevated Scale 5 along with an elevated Scale P.

4. A group of patients (*N*=52) with chronic, bilateral, noninflammatory, degenerative disease of the cornea (keratoconus) obtained a mean BR score of 67 on Scale 5, but were not significantly different from patients with other chronic eye diseases (Mannis, Morrison, Zadnick, Holland, & Krachmer, 1987).

5. Women who elected more conservative treatment for breast cancer, compared to women who elected mastectomy, obtained higher scores on the Narcissism scale, suggesting they valued their physical appearance more highly (Wolberg et al., 1987).

6. Retzlaff and Gibertini (1990) found this was the modal code of $N=124$ active-duty Air Force male personnel in an alcoholic rehabilitation program, at subclinical levels.

7. Cluster analysis found a group of alcoholics with a Spike 5' code (Retzlaff & Bromley, 1991), although this may have been the same sample as above.

Antisocial (6A) *Active Independent Type*

High scorers tend to show deficits primarily in the behavioral, social, and interpersonal domains.

These patients are quite narcissistic, fearless, pugnacious, daring, blunt, aggressive and assertive, irresponsible, impulsive, ruthless, victimizing, intimidating, dominating, often energetic, and competitive, but quite determined and independent. They are argumentative, self-reliant, revengeful, and vindictive. They are chronically dissatisfied and harbor resentments over people who challenge, criticize, or express disapproval over their behavior. They are characteristically touchy and jealous, brood over perceived slights and wrongs, and provoke fear in those around them through their intimidating social demeanor. They tend to present with an angry and hostile affect. They are suspicious and skeptical of the motives of other people, plan revenge for past grievances, and view others as untrustworthy. They avoid experiences of warmth, gentleness, closeness, and intimacy, viewing this as a sign of weakness. They often ascribe their own malicious tendencies onto the motives of others. They feel comfortable only when they have power and control over others. They are continually on guard against anticipated ridicule and act out in a socially intimidating manner, desiring to provoke fear in others and to exploit them for self-gain. These patients are driven by power, by malevolent projections, and by an expectation to anticipate suffering from others, so they react to maintain their autonomy and independence. Millon believes that their behavior is motivated by an expectancy that people will be rejecting and that other people are malicious, devious, and vengeful, thus justifying a forceful counteraction to maintain their own autonomy. They are alert for signs of ridicule and contempt, and react with impulsive hostility in response to felt resentments. They are prone toward substance abuse, relationship difficulties, vocational deficits, and legal problems.

Note. It is possible to have an antisocial character style without engaging in antisocial (criminal) behavior.

ROBERT J. CRAIG, PH.D.

Diagnosis. Antisocial Personality Disorder.

Subclinical. Independent, assertive, shrewd, competitive.

Research.

1. Antoni et al. (1985b) found that many patients with a 24/42 MMPI had elevated Scale 6A.

2. Cluster analysis of drug addicts treated in a therapeutic community found a group (*N*=55/235 [23%]) had a one-point 6A code. They had problems following program rules, stayed in treatment the fewest number of days, were less able to maintain abstinence among all patients who used drugs, and also relapsed faster (Fals-Stewart, 1992).

Aggressive/Sadistic (6B) *Active Discordant Type*

High-scoring patients manifest deficits primarily in interpersonal relationships. (The scale is a relatively pure measure of antagonism.)

These patients may not be publicly antisocial, but their clinical features are quite similar and the style may be considered as a more pathological variant of the Antisocial style. They engage in behaviors that are abusive and humiliating and that violate the rights and feelings of others. They are aggressive, forceful, fearless, commanding, militant, domineering, hardheaded, hostile, dominating, and intimidating personalities, pervasively destructive and brutal. They become combative when provoked and are antagonistic and disagreeable people. They tend to be touchy, excitable, and irritable and react angrily when confronted. In psychoanalytic terms, they are sadistic personalities. Some are able to sublimate these traits into socially approved vocations. When their autonomy is threatened, they are prone to spouse abuse and explosive outbursts that may result in legal problems.

Diagnosis. (DSM-III-R Appendix) Sadistic Personality Disorder.

Subclinical. An aggressive personality style.

Research.

1. Male spouse abusers (*N*=49) attained their highest scores on Scale 6B (Beasley & Stoltenberg, 1992).

Compulsive (7) (conforming) *Passive Ambivalent Type*

High scorers show deficits primarily in their behavior.

These patients are behaviorally rigid and constricted, conscientious, polite, organized, meticulous, punctual, respectful, often perfectionistic, formal, prudent, overconforming, cooperative, compliant with rules, serious, moralistic, self-righteous, self-disciplined, efficient, and relatively inflexible. They place high demands on themselves. They are emotionally restrained, suppressing their strong resentments and anger, and appear tense and grim but emotionally controlled. They are socially conforming and prone to a repetitive life-style, through adhering to a series of patterned behaviors and rules that must be followed. They have fears of social disapproval and are a model of propriety and restraint. They show excessive respect for authority, but may treat subordinates in an autocratic manner. They operate from a sense of duty that compels them not to let others down, thus risking the condemnation of authority figures. They thus show an anxious conformity. They strive to avoid criticism but expect it because of what they perceive to be their personal shortcomings. They fear making mistakes because of expected disapproval. Their behavior stems from a conflict between a felt hostility which they wish to express, and a fear of social disapproval should they expose this underlying oppositional resentment. This forces them to become overconforming, placing high demands on themselves which serve to control this intense anger, which occasionally breaks through into their behavior. Obsessive thinking may or may not be present.

Millon does not provide information on nor interpret low scale scores. However, a low score on Compulsive might suggest a lack of conformity and low impulse control.

Diagnosis. Obsessive-Compulsive Personality Disorder, or compulsive personality style, depending on the degree of severity and functional impairment.

Subclinical. Disciplined, orderly, organized, respectful, structured, virtuous, conforming, diligent, efficient, tidy.

Research.

1. Alcoholics with a Spike 7 have been found in cluster studies with alcoholics (Craig, Verinis, & Wexler, 1985 [*N*=23]); Donat, 1988; Donat, Walters, & Hume, 1991 [*N*=23]). Such patients tended to have attenuated drinking styles and had less severe complications associated with problematic drinking.

ROBERT J. CRAIG, PH.D.

2. Piersma (1987) found a group of male seminary students with a Spike 7 code. They were described as conscientious, self-disciplined, respectful, loyal, actively involved with others, and having a positive outlook on life.

3. Adams and Clopton (1990) found that high scores on Scale 7 among missionaries were associated with satisfaction with mission service and high self-esteem. Those who were more willing to question mission policies during missionary service had lower scores on Scale 7.

4. McCann (1992) found that the factor structure of Scale 7 assesses the components of sensation-seeking behavior, instability, and behavioral restraint. This is somewhat different from DSM-III-R criteria.

Caution. Several studies have found negative correlations (ranging from –.30 to –.42) between Scale 7 and DSM-III-R measures of the same construct. This suggests that this scale may be measuring something almost opposite to that depicted by DSM-III-R, and it suggests caution in ascribing an obsessive/compulsive diagnosis to elevated Scale 7 scores. Clinical work with this scale suggests that high-scoring patients are conscientious, rule-bound, and orderly. Thus they may have a compulsive *style* but not a compulsive *disorder*. Patients with an obsessive-compulsive personality disorder attain elevated BR scores on this scale, but high scores on Scale 7 do not automatically indicate an obsessive-compulsive personality disorder.

Passive-Aggressive (8A) (negativistic) *Active Ambivalent Type*

High scorers show deficits primarily in behavior and interpersonal relationships.

Millon believes that the conflicts of the active ambivalent type (passive-aggressive) are similar to those of the passive ambivalent type (compulsive), but are closer to consciousness and hence intrude into everyday behavior. The struggle between guilt and resentment permeates most aspects of their life.

These patients display a mixture of passive compliance and obedience at one moment and oppositional and negativistic behavior the next. They are moody, irritable, hostile, and manifest a grumbling and pessimistic demeanor. They are erratically and explosively angry and stubborn one moment and feel guilty and contrite the next moment. Disillusionment seems to permeate their lives. They feel misunderstood so they vacillate between passive dependency and stubborn contrariness that provokes discomfort and exasperation in those around them. They expect disappointment and maintain an unstable and conflictual role in relations with others. They sulk, feel unappreciated or feel they are being treated unfairly, constantly complain, and are persistently petulant and discontented. They often have problems with authority and, if employed, have job difficulties.

Commentary. Elevations in Scale 8A are a good indicator of problems with authority and with criminal behavior or potential for criminal behavior. Also, clinical elevations on this scale appear in a number of profile codes involving psychiatric patients. Patients with elevations on Scale 8A warrant close clinical evaluation.

Diagnosis. Passive-Aggressive Personality Disorder.

Note. Millon's passive-aggressive personality type is somewhat at variance with the DSM-III-R personality disorder with the same name. DSM-III-R criteria are defined around the single trait of a passive resistance to external demands. This is demonstrated in such behaviors as procrastination, dawdling, stubbornness, inefficiency, or purposeful "forgetfulness." Millon's version of this style is much broader, and the clinician should be alerted to this distinction when making the diagnosis. DSM-IV plans to introduce a "negativistic personality disorder," which is conceptually closer to Millon's active ambivalent style.

Subclinical. Temperamental, edgy, nagging.

Research.

1. Craig, Verinis, and Wexler (1985) found this pattern (with Scales C, P, and A also elevated) in 29/106 alcoholics in outpatient treatment.

2. Jay, Grove, and Grove (1987) found this code among a group of chronic pain patients. Scales A, D, and H were also significantly elevated in these patients.

3. Retzlaff and Gibertini (1990) found this to be the modal code (8ABT) among *N*=89 alcoholics in a VA inpatient rehabilitation program.

4. This was the modal code (8AC) among dropouts (*N*=12/28) from placebo-treated panic-disordered patients (Reich, 1990).

Self-Defeating (8B) *Passive Discordant Type*

High scorers show deficits primarily in interpersonal relationships.

These patients relate in a self-sacrificing, martyr-like manner, allowing others to take advantage of them. They seem to search for relationships in which they can lean on others for security and affection. Typically they act in an unassuming manner, denigrating themselves into believing they deserve their fate. Thus, this pattern is repeated in most relationships and therefore they are prone to be abused. It is conceptually similar to the analytic concept of masochism.

Diagnosis. (In DSM-III-R Appendix) Self-Defeating Personality Disorder (Masochistic personality).

Schizotypal (S) *Detached Dysfunctional Variant*

High scorers show deficits primarily in cognition and behavior.

This pattern represents a more severe dysfunctual variant of the schizoid or avoidant personality disorders.

These patients have behavioral peculiarities and eccentricities and seemed detached from the world around them, appearing strange and different. They tend to lead meaningless lives, drifting aimlessly from one activity to the next, remaining on the periphery of society. They are emotionally bland and tend to have flat affect, or perhaps an anxious wariness. They are socially detached and isolated and show a pervasive discomfort with others. They have few, if any, personal attachments and rarely develop any intimate relationships. Their thinking is irrelevant, tangential, disorganized, or autistic, and they suspiciously mistrust others. Cognitive confusion and perceptual distortions are the rule. They are self-absorbed and ruminative with feelings of derealization. They are prone to decompensate into schizophrenia if sufficiently stressed. Millon subdivides this disorder into two types: The active variant is characteristically anxious, wary, and apprehensive, while the passive type is characteristically emotionally bland.

Diagnosis. Schizotypal Personality Disorder.

Subclinical. Fragmented, suspicious, despondent.

Borderline (C) *Dysfunctional Variant*

High scorers manifest deficits in mood, relationships, and psychological spheres, particularly with their sense of identity.

These patients have conflicting and ambivalent feelings, intensely resenting those on whom they depend but yet preoccupied with maintaining their emotional support. They show persistent attachment disorders with patterns of intense but unstable relationships. They tend to experience intense but labile emotions—frequent mood swings with recurring periods of depression, anxiety, or anger followed by dejection and apathy. They often will present intense affect and with a history of impulsive behaviors. Manifestations of cheerfulness are often temporary cover-ups that mask deep fears of insecurity and fears of abandonment. They have strong dependency needs and are pre-occupied with seeking attention and emotional support and need considerable reassurance. These people are particularly vulnerable to separation from those who emotionally support them. Feelings of idealization are usually followed by feelings of devaluation, and there is considerable interpersonal ambiva-lence. They lack a clear sense of their own identity, and this uncertainty leads them to constantly seek approval, attention, and reaffirmation. Splitting and projective identification are their major defenses. They often have a punish-ing conscience and are prone to acts of self-mutilation and suicidal gestures. They are also prone to brief psychotic episodes and substance abuse.

Diagnosis. Borderline Personality Disorder.

Research.

1. Scale C (Mean BR=93.6) differentiated a group of 10 patients who made a suicide attempt from nonsuicidal depressed patients (Joffe & Regan, 1989b).

Paranoid (P) *Dysfunctional Variant*

High scorers manifest deficits primarily in behavior and thinking.

Millon believes that these patients are conflicted between issues of control and affiliation. They vigilantly mistrust others and have an abrasive, hostile, irritable, touchy, and irascible demeanor. They readily attack and humiliate anyone whom they perceive is trying to control them. They may become bel-ligerent, stemming from distorted cognitions or actual delusions. They tend to magnify interpersonal slights, are prone to distort events in order to support their own suspicions, and strongly resist external influence. They are fiercely independent and tend to be provocative in interpersonal relationships and to precipitate fear and exasperation in those around them. Their thinking is rigid and they often become argumentative. Projection is used as their main defense. They are particularly sensitive to perceived threats to their sense of self-determination. Delusions of grandeur, persecution, or ideas of reference may be present in the more extreme form of the disorder.

Diagnosis. Paranoid Personality Disorder.
(This style often covaries with the narcissistic, antisocial, and aggressive-sadistic personality styles.)

CLINICAL SYNDROMES

Anxiety Disorder (A)

High scorers are restless, anxious, apprehensive, tense, indecisive, unable to relax, edgy, and jittery. They have various somatic complaints related to physiological overarousal. These symptoms can include complaints of insomnia, muscular tightness, headaches, nausea, cold sweats, undue perspiration, clammy hands, and palpitations. Phobias may also be present, but more commonly symptoms are generalized. Behaviorally they have a sense of foreboding.

Commentary. This scale is elevated in anxiety, phobia, panic, and obsessional states, but it may not be able to distinguish between anxiety and depression, because the scale is often elevated in both conditions. It is a good measure, however, of psychic distress.

Diagnosis. Some form of Anxiety Disorder. Clinical judgment is required for a definitive pattern.

Somatoform Disorder (H)

High scorers are expressing psychological problems through somatic channels or have a legitimate physical illness but are coping so poorly with it that psychological reactions are compounding the manifestation of symptoms. They show persistent preoccupation with their poor health and often have symptoms in unrelated parts of the body. Symptoms are often expressed to gain attention and sympathy. Because their complaints are often nonresponsive to most forms of treatment, these patients tend to "doctor-shop," seeking cures but defeating intervention efforts. They make those around them miserable with their whining and complaining behavior.

Diagnosis. Somatoform Disorder or Psychological Factors Affecting Physical Condition.

Bipolar: Manic Disorder (N)

High scorers evince labile emotions, with frequent mood swings from elation to depression. During the manic phase they are restless, irritable, distractible, impulsive, and overactive with a flight of ideas, inappropriate enthusiasm, unrealistic goals, and a pressured and demanding quality in their interpersonal relations. Extremely high scores may also reflect psychotic processes with delusions and hallucinations.

Diagnosis. Bipolar Manic Disorder.

Dysthymic Disorder (D)

The high-scoring patient shows behavioral apathy, social withdrawal, low self-esteem, self-deprecatory comments, guilt, a pessimistic outlook toward the future, a lack of initiative, feelings of discouragement, guilt, a preoccupation with personal adequacy, and feelings of worthlessness. They are persistently sad, socially awkward, introverted, and plagued by self-doubts. They feel useless, have a diminished sense of pleasure, and feel a loss of self-confidence. Despite this, they are generally able to meet their daily responsibilities. Physical symptoms may include tearfulness, problems with concentration, either a poor or an excessive appetite, and perhaps suicidal ideation. Psychotic features are rarely present unless Scale CC is also elevated.

Diagnosis. Dysthymic Disorder.

Commentary. Because schizoid, avoidant, and dependent personality disorders may also present with a picture that seems dysthymic-like, these conditions should be ruled out as causative.

Alcohol Dependence (B)

High scores reflect current problematic drinking or a history of alcoholism along with subjective distress and problems in social, familial, and/or occupational functioning.

Diagnosis. Alcohol Abuse or Alcohol Dependence.

Commentary/Research. The research to date has found that alcoholics in treatment almost uniformly attain high scores on Scale B, averaging a BR score of 92 across these studies. However, these studies have all used alcoholics in treatment. No study has used the MCMI-II in a sample of patients who are motivated to hide their alcoholism. Thus, an elevated score reflects problematic drinking, but a low score on this scale does not necessarily preclude it. Also, the scale has good specificity and good sensitivity with primary alcoholics, but is less successful in identifying alcohol abuse among psychiatric patients (Craig & Weinberg, 1992a).

Drug Dependence (T)

High scores reflect both a person who has or has had a problem with drug dependence and the traits often associated with this behavior. These include hedonism, self-indulgence, impulsivity, exploitiveness, and a narcissistic personality. This is a person who has problems maintaining his or her daily affairs and is likely to experience considerable distress in social, occupational, familial, and legal areas.

ROBERT J. CRAIG, PH.D.

Diagnosis. Drug Abuse or Drug Dependence.
(Clinical evaluation needed to determine nature of specific drug abused.)

Commentary/Research. Studies to date with this scale have reported median BR scores into the 90s. However, all studies have used drug abusers already in residential or inpatient treatment. Such a population would have little reason to mask their drug abuse problem. No research has yet studied the ability of the scale to detect drug abuse in patients motivated to hide it (Craig & Weinberg, 1992b).

Thought Disorder (SS)

Elevated scores reflect persons whose thinking is disorganized, confused, fragmented, or bizarre. They often display inappropriate affect, with scattered hallucinations and unsystematized delusions. They usually are withdrawn, seclusive, and isolated; appear confused and disoriented; and feel misunderstood. They appear quite regressed.

Diagnosis. The following diagnoses are possible, depending on the length and course of the condition:

Brief Reactive Psychosis

Schizophreniform Disorder

Schizophrenia

Major Depression (CC)

High-scoring patients would be described as severely depressed with psychomotor depression or agitation, hopeless resignation from daily responsibilities, with feelings of worthlessness and guilt. Somatic symptoms may be present, including loss of appetite and weight, loss of energy, sleep disturbances, fatigue, and loss of sexual desire or drive. Suicidal ideation may be present. They brood incessantly and are pessimistic about the future. Their underlying personality style is most likely to be of the detached variety, especially dependent. They generally are incapable of normal daily functioning.

Diagnosis. Major Depression.

Commentary/Research. The research to date has tended not to support the validity of Scale CC. This scale does not contain items reflecting the vegetative signs that are required to establish the diagnosis, but rather those that pertain essentially to the cognitive signs of depression. Clinicians are advised to be cautious when using this scale to form a diagnosis involving Psychotic

---

Depression or Major Depression. However, the elevation of this scale in a profile provides good evidence of a depressive condition that requires clinical characterization.

Delusional Disorder (PP)

High scorers are usually considered actively paranoid with delusions of persecution or grandiosity. Their mood is usually hostile and they maintain a vigilance, suspiciousness, and alertness to those who are perceived as a threat. They may become belligerent and voice irrational ideas of reference, thought control, or thought influence.

Diagnosis. Delusional Disorder.

Appendix. DSM-IV plans to introduce a Depressive Personality Disorder, and Millon plans to add this to the next revision of the MCMI, the MCMI-III.

Depressive Personality

Patients with this personality style are quiet, introverted, passive, nonassertive, gloomy, pessimistic, serious, self-controlling, self-reproaching, self-derogatory, skeptical, hypercritical, hard to please, and they have difficulty having fun. Though generally responsible, conscientious, and self-disciplined, they tend to brood and worry, are preoccupied with negative events, and feel personally inadequate. People may exhibit these traits in the absence of a depressive disorder, but their personality style puts them at risk for developing a depressive disorder.

Diagnosis. Depressive Personality Disorder.

References for Chapters 2-4 appear at the end of Chapter 4.

4. Two-Point, Three-Point, and High-Ranging Codes

....

Scale 1 Codes

Most scores will include elevations on more than one personality disorder or clinical syndrome scale. The most common of these multiple configurations are described in this chapter. All configurations follow the same pattern: the scale with the highest score is listed first, followed by the second highest, then third highest, if applicable. Only BR scores >74 are included in the configurations, except where specifically indicated in the code descriptions. Elevated clinical syndrome scale scores—even if higher then personality disorder scale scores—are listed last in the configurations. Each description is followed by the DSM-III-R diagnosis and relevant research, if available. If clinicians encounter a configuration not described here, a suggested interpretation may be developed by integrating the individual scale descriptions found in Chapter 2.

12/21

These patients show dependent behaviors and tend to react to stress by withdrawing. They show a lack of initiative, have a low self-concept, and view themselves as weak, inadequate, and ineffectual. They tend to be socially alienated, are pervasively anxious and indecisive, and experience a state of chronic but moderate psychic stress. Obsessional thoughts may be present. They are most comfortable when alone. In the presence of others, they are passive and docile. Dynamics include a state of being uninterested in people; they are overly sensitive to rejection and hence view social situations as a source of anxiety. They are prone to separation anxiety and depression. (This code type is essentially identical to the Scale 1 one-point code description.)

Diagnosis. Schizoid Personality Disorder.

Research.

1. McNeil and Meyer (1990) reported that 12% of a forensic inpatient sample had this Schizoid/Avoidant pattern.

2. Concomitant MMPI codes have been reported as either a 28/82 (Antoni et al., 1985a) or a 78/87 (Antoni et al. 1987).

3. Cluster analysis found this code among *N*=89 alcoholics (Retzlaff & Bromley, 1991).

---

4. A cluster study found that 45/235 (19%) had this modal code among drug addicts treated in a therapeutic community. Given a program environment that fosters interpersonal closeness, these patients became self-critical, discouraged and dropped out of treatment more often than other types of patients. They also had worse outcomes, were less able to maintain abstinence, and relapsed faster (Fals-Stewart, 1992).

21 (P) (See 12 code type)

Research.

1. Josiassen, Shagass, and Roemer (1988) subdivided a group of 33 schizophrenics on the basis of their MCMI code types as reflecting "psychotic" or "nonpsychotic" schizophrenia. These two groups were found to differ on the amplitude of the somatosensory evoked potential EEGs. The nonpsychotic group had a 21 code type, while the psychotic group had a 21P code.

123

These patients have a weak ego and may become self-absorbed in daydreams that blur fantasy with reality. They seem pervasively depressed and appear sluggish and aloof. Their demeanor is characterized by a depressive blandness that masks a mix of inhibited anger, anxiety, and resentment. These patients show severe maladjustment with social apprehension, passivity, excessive compliance, blunted affect, and eccentric behavior. They are caught between feelings of loneliness and social apprehension. Their needs for closeness and affection are denied. They tend to search for supportive people or institutions who will take care of them. Unlike the personality style associated with 12/21 Code Type, these patients have far more dependency as an essential part of their personality. They avoid autonomous behaviors, suppress their anger and resentment toward their caretakers, and assume a passive, submissive, docile, and acquiescing role in relationships in order to fulfill their dependent needs. They are conciliatory, overly concerned with social rebuff, and prefer to maintain emotional distance in interpersonal relationships.

Diagnosis. Schizoid Personality Disorder with dependent traits.

Research.

1. Bartsch and Hoffman (1985) found this code among 31/123 inpatient alcoholics. For this group, drinking may medicate social anxiety to a level that produces self-assurance and permits reduced anxiety while in social contact. Their avoidant nature may make AA attendance problematic. Their MMPI code was 2478'.

123A

Millon (1983) reported that patients with this code experience prolonged periods of depressed or sad mood accompanied by social withdrawal, pessimism about the future, insomnia, early morning awakening, and other symptoms of depression. However, McMahon and Davidson (1985) suggest that, although this pattern often shows a code type associated with major depression, these patients also complain of tension, restlessness, and periods of fatigue and weakness with vague bodily complaints. These individuals have strong dependency needs, try to get these needs met, and, failing to do so, show emotional pain. They are hypersensitive to rejection which causes feelings of anger expressed in passive-aggressive ways so as to not alienate the person upon whom they depend. (Refer to the 123 code type and then add passive-aggressive features, traits, and behaviors.)

Research.

1. McCann and Suess (1988) found this code type among 25% of psychiatric inpatients, reflecting a schizoid, avoidant, dependent, and passive-aggressive blend of traits. Of these, 44% received a Diagnosis of Affective Disorder, 22% a Schizophrenic Disorder, 11% a Schizoaffective Disorder, 19% a diagnosis of some severe personality disorder, and 4% an Adjustment Disorder with Depressed Mood.

12345678A (subclinical) (e.g., all scales BR<70)

Research.

1. Tango and Dziuban (1984) found that this (subclinical) profile correlated with Strong-Campbell II vocational interests of athletics, public speaking, merchandising, and management among a population of college students seeking career counseling. They were called *nonstop drivers,* because they were people who wanted to be noticed. They had a driven quality about them and a need to conform to great expectations. Suspicious mistrust is the driving factor if they seek exhibitionistic roles. Striving for independence through the "top dog" position is seen.

128A

The personality style of these patients is comprised of introverted, avoidant, and negativistic features. They are not interested in interpersonal relations, tend to avoid social situations, and become negativistic and sullen when forced into social encounters. At the heart of their behavior is a belief that, if others got to know them, they would reject them. Not wanting to experience the attendant emotions, they react in a passive-aggressive manner to avoid such relationships and experiences.

Research.

1. Joffe and Regan (1989a) found this modal code among R=23 depressed patients who responded to tricyclic antidepressants.

12S

Suggests Schizotypal Personality Disorder. Refer to one-point code description for this disorder.

132

These people tend to prefer to remain by themselves, assume a passive stance, and avoid being the center of attention, yet they show apparent cooperativeness if they are unable to remain in the background. They tend to be viewed as agreeable and easygoing, though dull, apathetic, and detached. Fear of rejection is a likely dynamic to help understand their behavior.

Diagnosis. Consider Avoidant Personality Disorder.

136B78 (subclinical) (e.g., all scales < BR70)

Research.

1. Tango and Dziuban (1984) found that this (subclinical) profile correlated with Strong-Campbell II vocational interests of music and office practice among college students seeking career counseling. These people are called *retreaters*. They are pessimistic about the benefits of work and seem to prefer involvement in repetitive operations carried out under specific instructions. Career-choice indecision may signal discomfort with interpersonal contact and meaningful affiliations inherent in most kinds of work.

137

These patients show a combination of introverted and dependent traits, but also demonstrate rigid, formal, and compulsive traits that lend a disciplined aspect to their avoidance of people and indifference to social situations.

Diagnosis. Avoidant Personality Disorder.

138A

These people experience great discomfort when their dependency needs are threatened and are likely to become quite moody until their security is restored. Then they can once again assume behaviors characterized by passivity and acquiescence. Underlying feelings of anger are masked by their conciliatory behavior. This anger often will erupt through displays of temper or oppositional behaviors. When stressed they can become behaviorally erratic and emotionally labile.

Diagnosis. Dependent Personality Disorder with passive-aggressive traits.

153

These patients present as quiet, detached, ineffectual, apathetic, introverted, and dependent. Their affect is impoverished and they seem depressed and morose. Their thinking is confused, often marked by ideas of reference, magical thinking, and depersonalization. They seem eccentric, show deficits in social communication, and prefer a life of solitude, preferring a simple, repetitive, and dependent life-style. They occupy peripheral roles in most relationships. Their strongly ambivalent needs for dependency and their equally strong discontent and anger at their state in life is periodically displayed in hostility toward those on whom they depend for support.

17

These patients are introverted, dependent, distant, and emotionally controlled. They tend to be loners and prefer a life of solitude. They show little initiative or autonomous behaviors. Their affect is impoverished and they relate in a flat and apathetic manner. Social communication with these patients is quite difficult. They lack spontaneity, seem indifferent to their environment, and seem self-conscious when conversing with others. Their energy level is low and they seem constantly fatigued. They may display passive-aggressive behaviors when they become angry or discontented, but mostly they can be expected to lead a quiet, repetitive life, devoid of responsibilities and dependent on others to take care of them. They strive to be efficient, conscientious, orderly, dependable, and prepared so those in authority or those on whom they depend will value them, thereby maintaining the patient's safety and security. However, they prefer limited social contact. Anger probably underlies much of their affect.

Diagnosis. Schizoid Personality.

18A

These patients possess a self-image of being weak, inadequate, and ineffectual. They have low self-esteem and rarely initiate new activities. Their isolation reflects an indifference to social interaction rather than active disdain for or rejection of others. These patients tend to react to stress through emotional and behavioral withdrawal. Although they overtly display impoverished affect, they constantly worry under their bland exterior. If they are forced into situations that require social competence and interaction, they may become belligerent, oppositional, negativistic, and emotionally erratic. They may regress into a schizotypal pattern. (For further refinement, see one-point code descriptions for Schizoid and for Passive-Aggressive.)

Research.

1. Antoni et al., (1985b) found that many patients with this pattern had a 24/42 MMPI code.

18B2

These patients are characterologically introverted, apathetic, asocial, dependent, and timid. They avoid responsibility and prefer to remain in the background, leading relatively simple lives with repetitive behavior patterns and a slow personal tempo. They lack social initiative and act in a compliant and docile manner. Their affect is bland, but anger will occasionally be demonstrated, particularly when their routine is interrupted or when they are emotionally stressed. They maintain a peripheral role in most relationships and show a strong need to depend on others to fill their basic needs. They are quick to blame and belittle themselves and see themselves as weak and ineffectual. Erotic needs are likely weak. Thought processes are confused and tangential, making social communication very difficult. They are likely to appear depressed and seem unable to enjoy life. They show many self-defeating traits and behaviors.

ROBERT J. CRAIG, PH.D.

SCALE 2 CODES

213S

These patients are described as a fearfully dependent group. Their interpersonal style is both withdrawn and detached. Psychologically, their basic conflict is the simultaneous existence of strong dependency needs and a fearful mistrust of others. These persons intensely long for affection from others, but expect rejection and hostility so strongly that they have major difficulties in relating interpersonally. Their behavior is usually characterized by a demeanor that appears helpless, inferior, and inadequate. This behavioral style helps them avoid rejection and humiliation. However, such withdrawal only intensifies their unmet needs for affection and thereby perpetuates this pathological pattern. When they do relate interpersonally, they develop very tenuous attachments, assuming a passive and submissive role. Autonomous behaviors are held in check for fear of eliciting rebuke. Outwardly, they often appear bland and aloof, although this exterior frequently masks underlying anxieties and resentments. Their self-image is one of self-devaluation and low self-esteem. They may regress to a more schizotypal variant.

Research.

1. Levine, Tischer, Antoni, Green, & Millon (1985) found that many in this group had a 27/72 MMPI code.

2138A

Research.

1. Using cluster analysis, Mayer and Scott (1988) found this code among 15/112 (12%) male inpatient alcoholics. This code suggests chronic pathology in personality structure with transient psychotic episodes with bizarre behavior. Patients in this cluster were also significantly less likely to complete treatment.

218A

These patients show behavior that is characterized by eccentricities and autistic thinking. They seem lost in their own thoughts, fantasies, and daydreams. Their thinking is tangential and they communicate in strange speech patterns. They do not trust others and may feel persecuted, so they tend to withdraw and assume a detached appearance. A basic problem for them, however, is that they also have strong dependency needs. Unable to function independently, they are forced to rely on the very people they also mistrust to take care of them. They require dependable caretakers or institutions to maintain their needs. They are quite passive dependent. They rarely show emotions, except anger when pressured. Otherwise, they behave in a passive-aggressive manner.

Diagnosis. Schizotypal Personality.

Research.

1. This was the modal code among a group of both white (*N*=149) and black (*N*=109) male schizophrenics in a VA hospital. The patients were considered "symptom reporters," and hence the MCMI was able to "detect" their pathology. When the group was subdivided into patients who did not report their pathology, the test was less successful in detection of schizophrenia (Jackson, Greenblatt, Davis, Murphy, & Trimkus, 1991).

23/32

These patients tend to react to stress with inwardly directed anger and frustration. Their essential psychological conflict is strong dependency needs combined with an equally strong fear of independence and an extreme mistrust of others. This results in chronic psychic tension. They are fearful of rejection from those whose assistance they require for support, and they may withdraw from their only source of reinforcement, resulting in a life of loneliness and social isolation. Occasionally they tolerate people in order to get needed sources of support, but only for short durations, because this results in much discomfort due to their continuing distrust. They view life as empty and emotionally draining. Their affective state is generally composed of anxiety, sadness, anger, and frustration. Millon believes that the inability to resolve this conflict may culminate in a decompensation to either a schizotypal pattern, a borderline pattern, or both.

Research.

1. McNeil and Meyer (1990) found that 15% of forensic inpatients were Avoidant/Dependent.

2. Many patients with this code type had a 28/82 MMPI code type (Antoni et al., 1985a) or a 78/87 MMPI code type (Antoni et al., 1987).

3. Joffe, Swinson, and Regan (1988) found this code among 23 patients with primary obsessive-compulsive disorder reflecting a mixed personality disorder with avoidant, dependent, and passive-aggressive features.

4. (23C) Bryer, Nelson, Miller, and Krol (1987) found this code among a sample of 14 women who were hospitalized in a psychiatric unit with a history of sexual abuse. The diagnosis was Borderline.

231

These people feel inadequate and constantly afraid that others will reject them. Therefore, they feel tense and nervous in interpersonal situations and adopt the response style of an introvert. They are likely to have few friends because they tend to negatively compare themselves with others and hence make little effort to develop intimate social contacts. (See Code Type 23 for more descriptors.)

2318A

In addition to the descriptors associated with the 23 and 231 Code Types, these patients also have, as part of their personality structure, a streak of oppositional negativistic behaviors that are manifested only when stressed or when social or interpersonal demands requiring independent action are placed upon them.

Diagnosis. Consider Schizotypal Personality with avoidant, dependent, and passive-aggressive traits.

238A

Millon theorizes that the behavior of these patients emanates from a conflict between the desire to withdraw and an equally intense fear of independence. The inability to resolve this conflict results in emotional turmoil, chronic psychological stress, avoidant behaviors, and much apprehension and anxiety in social encounters. They fear acting independently because of their self-doubts, because they fear rejection, and because they feel they cannot depend on others, again due to their intense mistrust. They often act in a negativistic or passive-aggressive manner, which often elicits the very rejection they expect from others. Psychologically, they are repeatedly discontented and may show frequent outbursts. Their anger is contained by withdrawing and becoming anxiously depressed.

Diagnosis. Consider Avoidant Personality with passive-aggressive traits.

Research.

1. Bryer et al. (1987) found this code among a sample of 14 women with histories of physical and sexual abuse, assessed while on an inpatient psychiatric unit.

238B

These patients are fearful and dependent. They lean on others for security and assume the role of a submissive and self-sacrificing partner in close relationships. They become very insecure when threatened with loss of support, so they place themselves in an inferior or demeaning position, thus allowing others to exploit and abuse them. They may seek out relationships in which they will suffer. They have an intense need for affection and nurturance, and, though often resentful of those on whom they lean, they fear expressing those hostilities, which would risk their emotional security. Such feelings may be expressed in a passive-aggressive manner, if at all. Because they are fearful of social rejection, they assume a self-sacrificing role in relationships and would rather withdraw than vent their anger directly. The price they usually pay for this behavior is a combination of depression, loneliness, and isolation. It is their insecurity and fear of abandonment that leads them to appear submissive and to suppress all resentments. They act in a conciliatory, placating, and ingratiating manner, assuming the role of a weak and helpless victim. They express a lack of self-confidence and low self-esteem and act in a self-depriving manner in order to attain or continue to receive assurance and support. They thus are subject to abuse and intimidation. Although this is painful, it is not as painful as total abandonment.

Diagnosis. Consider Avoidant, Dependent or Self-Defeating Personality Disorder, or a Mixed Personality Disorder featuring these traits.

23S

These patients are characterized by a withdrawal from social encounters, emotional isolation, an apprehensive and guarded exterior, surface apathy, dependent relationships, an indifference to social surround, suppression of feelings and emotions, self-depreciation, confused thinking, feels of depersonalization, peculiar and hallucinatory-like sensations, episodes of derealization, bizarre behaviors, eccentricities (superstitious, magic, and occult), excessive social anxiety with unfamiliar people, a variety of odd beliefs, constricted affect, and an undue suspiciousness.

These patients are at risk for decompensation into a psychotic disorganization when stressed. Their use of withdrawal and social isolation as coping defenses is not completely effective, and their protective detachment can become deficient, resulting in chaotic and primitive impulses and psychosis.

Diagnosis. Schizotypal Personality Disorder.

25

These people fear rejection and humiliation while also overvaluing their sense of self-worth. They believe they have special abilities or qualities that set them apart from others; they therefore believe that others would reject them because of these special abilities. This provides the rationalization for their social withdrawal. They are at risk for depression.

26A

These patients are mistrusting, suspicious, competitive, and self-reliant. They view others as weak and deserving of exploitation and try to take advantage of them. They are impulsive and intimidating and may become cruel and malicious. This outward behavior may actually mask a fear of underlying dependence.

Research.

1. This was the modal profile for a group of black, male psychiatric patients (N=34) described as angry but nonpsychotic (Greenblatt & Davis, 1992).

28A (see also 8A2)

This pattern combines the features of avoidant and negativistic traits. These patients are sensitive to rejection, uncomfortable in social situations, become nervous in interpersonal situations, and tend to be loners. If they are able to establish a permanent relationship, it is likely to be conflictual, largely due to the patients' vacillating between behavior that is friendly and cooperative and behavior that is negativistic, hostile, and obstructionistic. They are sensitive to perceived criticism or censure, may frequently misinterpret others as critical, and are prone to sudden outbursts of anger. Embarrassment after such outbursts may result in a depression and a withdrawal form social contact.

Research.

1. Cluster analysis found this code for N=60 alcoholics (Donat, 1988; Donat, Walters, & Hume, 1991).

2. This was the modal profile of a group of black, male psychiatric patients (N=66) described as non-angry and psychotic (Greenblatt & Davis, 1992).

3. This was the modal code among inpatient psychiatric patients (N=150) with mixed diagnoses (Murphy, Greenblatt, Mozdzierz, & Trimakas, 1990).

28A3

This pattern suggests an avoidant personality with passive-aggressive and dependent features. It describes people who desire detachment from others and fear independence. The tension that is created by this conflict may result in chronic resentment and even an open petulance with a passive-aggressive quality. These patients feel chronically misunderstood and unappreciated. They constantly fear that their dependency security is in jeopardy. Therefore they become discontented and moody, and they engage in outbursts that evoke negative reactions in others. This becomes a kind of self-fulfilling prophecy that reinforces their withdrawal and increases anxiety. Their self-doubts only inhibit self-initiated actions.

Diagnosis. Consider Avoidant Personality with passive-aggressive traits.

28A71

These patients are hostile, distrustful, demanding, negativistic, oppositional, and faultfinding, and they carry a "chip-on-the-shoulder" attitude. They view themselves as weak, inadequate, and ineffectual. They believe they have been repeatedly rejected but yet they are motivated by a need for power, so they may act aggressively. They want to relate in a less hard-boiled manner, but they are so sensitive to signs of rejection that any easing in their tension is likely to be short-lived. Much passive-aggressive behavior can be expected. Additionally, there is a compulsive and repetitive aspect to their behavior.

28A8B

This pattern emphasizes negativistic, self-defeating, and avoidant/dependent traits.

Research.

1. McCann and Gergelis (1990) found this as the modal profile among a group of 40 psychiatric inpatients who had made suicide attempts. The code type reflects emotional dysfunction in the form of angry and depressive affect with feelings of helplessness and inability to adequately cope. However, there were no MCMI-II differences between those with suicidal ideation and those who had made a suicidal attempt.

28B

These patients are constantly apprehensive that people will reject them. Although they desire to relate and want acceptance, they feel it is better to maintain an emotional distance in their relationships. They often display a surface apathy to hide their excess sensitivities and concerns about rejection. They believe that their security will be threatened should they express felt resentments, so they continually minimize the hostility they both feel and expect. Much of their behavior has a self-defeating aspect to it. They may act in such a way as to elicit or provoke rejection and even abuse, thereby reinforcing their beliefs and fears. This tends to result in withdrawal and dysphoria.

Diagnosis.

1. Consider Personality Disorder Not Otherwise Specified, with self-defeating and avoidant traits.

2. If Scale S is also elevated, consider Schizotypal Personality Disorder.

28B88A

This pattern emphasizes self-defeating and passive-aggressive traits with avoidant behavior.

Research.

1. This was the modal code for a group (N=16) of patients with a diagnosis of multiple personality disorder (Fink & Golinkoff, 1990).

32 (see 23 code)

These people are self-effacing, noncompetitive, and constantly seek relationships in which they rely on others for guidance and security. They tend to show both dependent and avoidant traits. They tend to become dependent on institutional, if not personal, sources of support.

Research.

1. Kennedy, McVey, and Katz (1990) found this to be a modal code among 44 eating-disordered females (inpatients). A borderline personality diagnosis was particularly prevalent in the bulimic group (N=16) and remained so after treatment.

2. This was the modal profile for a group of white, male psychiatric patients (N=185) described as non-angry and psychotic (Greenblatt & Davis, 1992).

Scale 3 Codes

321

These patients are likely to have become accustomed to a dependent state with chronically flat affect. They have low self-esteem and feel inadequate. They are passive, dependent, submissive, and acquiescent. They are apprehensive in social situations and strive to be cooperative in order to establish and maintain a protective relationship on someone else. They are at risk for separation anxiety if they perceive they are about to be abandoned.

3218A

In addition to the traits associated with the 321 code type, these patients are also passive-aggressive, negativistic, socially withdrawn, and easily discouraged. They view themselves internally as powerless and inadequate and tend to show few coping resources.

Research.

This code was found among 35/195 (18%) psychiatric inpatients (Donat et al., 1992).

327

These patients tend to be cooperative followers, taking a passive and dependent role in relationships and constantly seeking emotional support through their acquiescence. They have low self-esteem and are frequently lonely and isolated. They defend against feelings of insecurity through compulsive-like behaviors characterized by persistence, compliance, orderliness, and dependability, all designed to maintain security.

328A

This pattern reflects people who display stubbornness, passive-aggression, and periodic irritable outbursts, but who otherwise are cooperative, conciliatory, and dependent. Negativistic behaviors may be expressed covertly through an uncooperativeness or overtly through constant complaining. However, they tend to avoid competitive situations that would threaten their security.

Research.

1. Joffe and Regan (1991) found this to be the modal code among a group of 20 patients with an affective disorder whose family history was negative for depression. These findings are consistent with the psychoanalytic literature which suggests that obsessional and dependent traits may predispose patients to depression.

2. Piersma (1986) found this code among a sample of 151 admissions to a private psychiatric hospital. Of these, 85% had a clinical diagnosis of Affective Disorder (most common was Major Depression) and the remainder had Adjustment Reactions or Anxiety Disorders.

3. Craig, Verinis, and Wexler (1985) found this pattern in 23/106 outpatient alcoholics.

34

These patients are submissive, dependent, obliging, and overcompliant, and are preoccupied with seeking approval to maintain their security. This behavior stems from a fear of losing emotional support. They accommodate to and respond to the needs and wishes of others, having learned to assume an inferior role in relationships. However, unlike a passive dependent person, these patients actively seek reassurance and praise through the use of charm, self-dramatizing behaviors, seductiveness, or expressive emotion that will also bring them approval and affection. Their suppressed emotions may suddenly erupt despite their efforts to control their oppositional feeling. Millon theorizes that felt resentments stem, in part, from their awareness that they have little or no identity apart from others. Therefore, they seek to minimize any signs of disapproval.

345

These patients show a mixture of dependent and histrionic traits. In addition to the passive dependency, the reliance on others to take care of them, the need for constant reassurance, and the fear of disapproval seen in dependent personality styles, this code type also indicates that patients actively seek attention in a socially gregarious manner such as that which is seen in patients who are histrionic. Their basic motivation is to receive approval and praise. Millon believes that underneath this behavior are fears of abandonment that cause them to seek relationships with people who will accept their submissive and approval-seeking behaviors.

Diagnosis. Consider Dependent Personality with histrionic traits.

3457

These patients have a mixture of dependent, histrionic, narcissistic, and compulsive traits.

Research.

1. Tango and Dziuban (1984) found that this (subclinical) profile correlated with the Strong-Campbell II vocational interests in adventure, music, writing, religion, public speaking, and office management among college students seeking career counseling. They were termed as *uncommitted proprietors* who had intrusive intentions toward work but lacked persistence or depth. They expressed strong desires to be in a proprietorship with somewhat exhibitionistic roles (writer, orator, executive, merchant, adventurer, musician). They have a flirtatious and uncommitted sociability, immature sensation-seeking tendency, and interpersonal exploitiveness. Career indecision may reflect fear of commitment.

348A

These patients are essentially dependent personalities with all attendant traits. They may demonstrate histrionic behaviors to cover up their fears of abandonment in order to maintain their security. Unlike other MCMI code types that suggest dependency, these patients are also quite moody, behaviorally erratic, and oppositional, particularly when their security is threatened. Often these patients behave in a querulous and fault-finding way to test the faithfulness of those on whom they rely. Millon believes that low self-esteem underlies their behavior and that they need to conceal this by acting in a self-assured manner.

Diagnosis. Personality Disorder Not Otherwise Specified, dependent, histrionic, and passive-aggressive traits.

35

Millon theorizes that the behavior suggested by this code type results from a conflict between dependence and a fear of independence. Their fear of abandonment compels them to be submissive and compliant, constantly seeking reassurance to protect their source of security. However, they resent their caretakers and need to suppress this, lest they experience rejection and loss of support. In addition to their passive and submissive behaviors, they also have

---

narcissistic qualities that suggest feelings of entitlement, a requirement for constant attention, and preoccupation with themselves. They have erratic and variable moods, occasional angry outbursts, and negativistic and oppositional behavior, particularly when forced toward independent behaviors. When their dependency security is threatened, they may become remorseful, contrite, disparaging, and obliging, all designed to recapture their security.

Diagnosis. Dependent Personality Disorder, with narcissistic and passive-aggressive traits.

356A

These people behave in a cooperative and congenial manner, but also believe they have special abilities and therefore deserve special treatment and attention. Though emotionally dependent, they try to act independently or try to control others. They are at risk for problems with substance abuse.

357

The behavior of these patients consists of cooperativeness in order to secure guidance and protection from a stronger interpersonal figure. They tend to rationalize failures and to portray themselves in an overly positive light. They can be expected to be proper and respectful, hard-working, disciplined, and controlled to avoid letting people see their low self-esteem.

36A

Millon theorizes that the behavior of these patients arises from an intense conflict between dependence and a fear of independence. The inability to resolve this conflict results in continued anxiety in social contexts. They act in a conciliatory and congenial manner to maintain security, and they tend to rely on others or on institutions for support. When their security is threatened, they may become hostile, aggressive, impulsive, moody, negative, and prone to act out their emotions. They believe that people will take advantage of them and so they must be alert to their fears of being controlled. When stressed by these beliefs, they can become intimidating; when their security is returned, they will resume their obliging and acquiescing manner.

37

These patients are tense, rigid, organized, and efficient, and characteristically behave in a weak, passive, or ingratiating way. They have low self-esteem and a strong need to rely on one or two people. The failure to meet their needs occasionally results in the breakthrough of hostile feelings. It is critical for these patients to court approval and acceptance and avoid disapproval and anticipated disfavor.

Diagnosis. Dependent or Compulsive Personality Disorder.

Research.

1. Hamberger and Hastings (1986) found this code among 16/99 males in a domestic violence abatement program.

2. Jay, Grove and Grove (1987) found this pattern among a group of chronic headache patients.

3. Joffe and Regan (1991) found this as the modal code among 20 affectively disordered patients in remission, whose family history was negative for depression.

372

These patients are submissive, dependent, docile, obliging, and self-effacing. They assume a passive, compliant role in relationships and rely on others for guidance, approval, and security. Although they resent their caretakers, this resentment is not able to be expressed, lest they experience disfavor and rejection. The resentment is therefore hidden by overtly proper behavior. Insecurity and fears of abandonment underlie their surface appearance of a quiet, submissive, and benign personality. They are at risk for separation anxiety and subsequent depression. Though generally cooperative and conscientious, they fear making mistakes that would elicit disapproval. Demands for independence heighten their insecurity, increase anxiety, and result in even more compulsive defenses. Hence, this pattern is ingrained and relatively intransigent. They like to give the impression of being content, so they are reluctant to report any psychological discomfort.

Diagnosis. Consider Schizoid or Dependent Personality Disorder with compulsive traits.

38A

This pattern shows an interpersonal ambivalence, a discontented self-image, irritable affectivity, explosive anger, and oppositional behavior. These patients are dependent and sensitive to rejection, disapproval, or loss of favor, so they maintain a dependent stance in relationships to secure acceptance and nurturance. They feel insecure and are vulnerable to threats of separation. When their security is threatened, they may become negativistic, querulous, uncooperative, passive-aggressive, petulant, or even aggressive until they secure a haven which will take care of them.

Research.

1. Cluster analysis found this code among alcoholics (N=89) (Retzlaff & Bromley, 1991).

38A2

Refer to code type 38A for personality description, and then add avoidant features, social anxiety, withdrawal, and sensitivity to rejection as part of the description.

Research.

1. Joffe & Regan (1989a) found this as the modal code among (N=19) depressed patients who did not respond to tricyclic antidepressants.
2. This was the modal pattern among alcoholic women in treatment with enduring depression (N=15) (McMahon & Tyson, 1990).

38B

These patients have the essential features of both dependent and self-defeating personality traits, with the latter predominating. Refer to one-point code descriptions for Scale 8B and then add the dependent features to the description (see Scale 3).

Note. Clinicians must be careful to evaluate whether this behavior is a result of a personality style or a disorder, and whether it is a reaction to living in a chronically abusive and hopeless situation where patients have learned to be helpless (e.g., Battered Wife Syndrome—if applicable).

SCALE 4 CODES

Diagnosis. Self-Defeating Personality Disorder. Masochistic (in an analytic sense).

43

These patients have features of both dependent and histrionic personality traits. They are dependent on others for attention, affection, and security and will act either submissively dependent and cooperative or in an attention-seeking, overly dramatic manner in order to maintain approval. Millon theorizes that they fear abandonment and so act in an obliging and accommodating—even seductive—way to maintain their security relationships. However, this dynamic is largely outside patients' awareness. They are prone to unstable emotionality and impulsive and angry outbursts when they feel rejected or fall into disfavor from valued situations or relationships.

43C

Emphasize Borderline personality traits (See Scale C).

Diagnosis. Borderline Personality Disorder, dependent type.

438A

The behavior of these patients is characterized by surface emotionality, loud and boisterous affirmations of their beliefs, and exhibitionistic, dramatic, and attention-seeking traits. Millon theorizes that their underlying conflict is a sense of low self-esteem, which they mask with a social demeanor that appears confident and self-assured. They may appear to be cooperative and compliant, but may show their resistance covertly. They may become angry and verbally aggressive when they do not receive sufficient attention. They are prone to act in a negativistic and oppositional manner when stressed; otherwise, they use their charm and seductiveness to seek attention and favor.

45

These patients are essentially narcissistic. They seek praise and attention, have an inflated sense of self-worth, and are quite sociable but indifferent to social responsibility and to the welfare of others. They are superficially charming, but their interpersonal relationships are usually shallow and manipulative; they demand self-praise. They will provide attention to others as long as it brings attention to themselves. Though they may make a good impression on others, those more intimate with them see their deceptions and unreliability. They fend off attacks with anger and self-dramatizing behaviors. They constantly behave so as to draw attention to themselves.

Diagnosis. Narcissistic Personality Disorder.

Research.

1. A 45' modal code was found in a group of normal subjects (*N*=18) and a group of sons of alcoholics (*N*=13), all with high EEG alpha waves, suggesting a positive relationship between high alpha and extroverted personality traits (Wall, Schuckit, Mungas, & Ehlers, 1990).

2. This code was found among 40/235 (17%) addicts treated in a therapeutic community (Fals-Stewart, 1992).

4537 (BR 60 - 75)

These people are often well-functioning individuals, perhaps undergoing periods of stress. They are outgoing, but tend to be self-centered and dramatic, soliciting praise and recognition. They seem charming and affable, but intimate acquaintances can attest to abrupt and angry outbursts and some exploitation within the family. They often present with marital difficulties.

456A

This pattern suggests individuals who are self-centered, narcissistic, dramatic, confident, and superficially friendly but who deal with people in a demanding, manipulative, and often intimidating fashion, particularly to get attention. Essentially they are undependable and have shallow interpersonal relationships. Resentment and hostility are readily projected onto others. They can be charming, but they are also overly sensitive and tend to react abrasively. They are self-reliant and unlikely to willingly enter into a therapeutic alliance.

Diagnosis. Antisocial Personality Disorder is the most likely diagnosis.

Research.

1. Bartsch and Hoffman (1985) found this pattern in a group of 23/125 inpatient alcoholics. Drinking for these patients might be recreational or a manifestation of a life-style of self-indulgence and thrill seeking. Their MMPI profile was a 49' code.

2. Retzlaff and Gibertini (1987) found this code (in subclinical ranges) among a group of Air Force pilot trainees. They were described as

arrogant, dramatic, excitable, easily bored with routine tasks, and at times erratic and impulsive. They were bold and adventurous, but possibly prone to unreflective responsiveness and poor judgment. They displayed a supreme nonchalance and imperturbability.

3. Donat (1988) and Donat, Walters, and Hume (1991) found this code for *N*=14/150 alcoholics.

4. A group of adult children of alcoholics (*N*=15) had this as the modal code, along with an elevated Scale C (Hibbard, 1989).

457

Emphasize narcissistic traits with dramatic and attention-seeking behaviors.

Research.

1. Retzlaff and Gibertini (1987) found this cluster among a group of Air Force pilot trainees in subclinical ranges. They were perceived as dominant, achieving, enduring, affiliating and orderly. Thrill-seeking and playfulness were low and they assumed a matter-of-fact, highly structured approach to coping. They were seen as levelheaded.

458A

These patients show a prominent need for attention and may engage in thrill-seeking and adventurous behaviors in order to get it. They may appear charming, though dramatic and colorful. They act in a confident and self-assured manner and become disdainful when questioned. These patients tend to become angry, negativistic, provocative, aggressive, or hostile.

46A8A

These patients enjoy being the center of attention and act in a dramatic, colorful, and flourishing manner to acquire the attention they seek. They view the world as essentially competitive, and they are constantly vigilant in case others try to take advantage of them. They are conflicted because they desire attention yet do not trust others. Hence these patients may become resistant and distant, or they may erupt in explosive anger or aggression. Others may act passive-aggressively, appearing to superficially comply but actually being obstructionistic.

47

These patients thrive on seeking attention by being dramatic, exciting, and even charismatic. They tend to make a positive first impression but become easily bored. However, they value the compulsive type of life-style and try to be efficient, conscientious, dependable, and persistent. They are constantly struggling to express their emotions or to control them—to act in silly ways or to follow the rules of social propriety. This tends to make them emotionally labile. Millon theorizes that this behavior hides a fear of autonomy.

Diagnosis. Histrionic Personality Disorder.

48A

These patients appear sociable, affable, friendly, obliging, and even charismatic, but they also engage in dramatic and attention-seeking behaviors. Millon believes that this personality type has an intense fear of true autonomy. Beneath their social facade and apparent self-confidence are feelings of inadequacy and resentments that they try to suppress. However, they are not good at controlling their negativistic and oppositional tendencies, which frequently erupt in dramatic, verbal attacks. If employed, they are likely to appear organized and efficient and court the favor of their superiors, having a strong need to feel appreciated. Should they not express their anger, they could be prone to developing psychosomatic disorders due to the vitriolic nature of their personality style which, if suppressed, would be displaced onto organ systems.

Diagnosis. Histrionic Personality Disorder.

48A6A

These patients have the personality characteristics described in the 48A code type, but also have antisocial traits. Problems with alcohol or drugs are commonly seen in patients with this profile.

Diagnosis. Mixed Personality Disorder with histrionic, passive-aggressive, and antisocial traits.

SCALE 5 CODES

52

These patients feel superior to others and accordingly believe they are due special attention. They exaggerate their own self-worth and become enraged

---

when they believe others are devaluing them in any way (refer to Scale 5 one-point code description for further elaboration). However, these patients are more dependent than the pure narcissist and more sensitive to rejection.

53

These patients highly value themselves and relate with an air of self-assurance, but the addition of dependency traits in the personality indicate that they are actually very unsure of themselves and their own abilities. This results in vacillating styles of relating, from being congenial and cooperative to being dominant and assertive (refer to Scale 5 one-point code description for further elaboration).

Research.
1. This was the modal code among 800 male adjudicated felons evaluated as part of a sentence reconsideration program in a state diagnostic and reception center (Ownby, Wallbrown, Carmin, & Barnett, 1991).

534

These patients are narcissistic, manipulative, gregarious, and superficially charming, and use self-dramatization and seductiveness as a means of gaining attention, admiration, and support. They have underlying dependency needs, which are denied. When their dependency security is threatened they may react with anger, resentment, and hostility. Casual observers may judge them as friendly and sociable, but more intimate acquaintances can attest to their unreliability, lack of empathy, impulsiveness, and resentment whenever they do not get their way. Most relationships in their lives are shallow and do not last. They rarely are loyal, unless it meets their own self-interests. Some patients with this code type are prone to antisocial tendencies.

Diagnosis. Narcissistic Personality Disorder.

Research.
1. Hamberger and Hastings (1986) found this code among 11/99 males in a domestic violence abatement program.

536A

These patients show the personality traits associated with a 53 code type. However, they also have antisocial traits as part of their personality. In addition to their narcissistic qualities, they can become angry, resentful, hostile, vindictive, and vengeful when crossed or when they perceive that people are not providing them with sufficient attention. They are prone to impulsive temper tantrums and outbursts that may include violence.

Diagnosis. Narcissistic and/or Antisocial.

54

These patients overvalue their abilities and talents. They expect others to consider them special and therefore more deserving of attention and praise. They may appear conceited and arrogant. Underneath this behavior is a strong need for approval, so that they behave with a dramatic flair to draw attention to themselves. They need constant admiration.

Diagnosis. Narcissistic Personality Disorder.

Research.

1. Drug addicts (N=144) (mostly cocaine abusers) in residential treatment attained this modal code (Yeager, DiGuiseppe, Resweber, & Leaf, 1992).

2. In subclinical ranges, Retzlaff and Gibertini (1987b; 1988) found this code to characterize Air Force officers in pilot training. They show predominant histrionic and narcissistic personality patterns and were seen as highly sociable with strong self-esteem. They were levelheaded and well-adjusted.

546A

In addition to the traits associated with a narcissistic personality type (see Scale 5 one-point code description), these patients have histrionic and antisocial character traits that are a prominent part of their behavior. This includes an air of self-assuredness, confidence, arrogance, conceit, and competitiveness. They enjoy and are skillful at manipulating and exploiting the naive, and engage in deceptive or seductive and dramatizing behaviors to get others to do their bidding. They can be intimidating, and lack empathy. When they experience a perceived narcissistic injury, they may respond with anger or vindictive behavior. They may manifest sexual excesses, substance abuse, violent histories, and other forms of acting out. Marital conflicts are also common.

Diagnosis. Consider Mixed Personality Disorder with narcissistic and antisocial traits.

Research.

1. McMahon and Davidson (1986) found this code among a group of alcoholics without depression.

2. Cluster analysis has found this code among alcoholics (Donat, 1988; Donat, Walters, & Hume, 1991; Retzlaff & Bromley, 1991).

3. A cluster study of drug addicts in a therapeutic community found that 52/235 (22%) had this as a modal code (Fals-Stewart, 1992).

548A

In addition to the traits described in the 54 code type and further elaborated on in the one-point code of the Narcissist (Scale 5), these patients respond to narcissistic injuries with negativistic, passive-aggressive, and obstinate behaviors. Emotionally, they become resentful and erratic. Anger is the most frequently seen emotional expression. Patients with this profile are at risk for substance abuse, sexual excess, and other forms of acting-out behavior.

56A

Millon's theory classifies these types as an emotionally acting-out group. These patients demonstrate the combined features of the Narcissistic and Antisocial personality styles. Millon believes people with this personality type are driven by fear and mistrust of other people and fiercely defend their independence. Descriptors applicable in the Narcissistic (Scale 5) and Antisocial (Scale 6) scales are applicable in describing this type. Interpersonally, they are intimidating, vindictive, menacing, threatening, provocative, and vigilant to signs of attempts to control them. They are also conceited, attention seeking, and lack empathic skills. Relationships are shallow, because they cannot trust others and because of their controlling and vindictive qualities. Marital and family problems, substance abuse, and legal problems often occur with this code type.

Diagnosis. Antisocial personality type, or Antisocial Personality Disorder if associated with delinquent acts, or Narcissistic Personality Disorder, or both.

Research.

1. Hamberger and Hastings (1986) found this code in 14/99 males in a domestic violence abatement program. These patients were described as self-centered, rigid in insisting their values and rules be accepted, used others to meet their own needs, and reciprocated only when it met their advantage. They felt entitled to be treated differently from others. Any hesitation or refusal by others to respond to their demands invited threats and aggression. Their DSM-III diagnosis was Narcissistic Personality Disorder.

2. Craig, Verinis, and Wexler (1985) found this cluster in a sample of outpatient alcoholics.

3. Antoni et al. (1986) found that many patients with this code had an 89/98 MMPI code.

4. McNeil and Meyer (1990) report that 11% of forensic inpatients and 37% of a correctional inmate sample with this code were Narcissistic and Antisocial.

5. Corbisiero and Reznikoff (1991) found this cluster among 24/247 alcoholics. This group showed less psychopathology, had a less compulsive style of use, and fewer adverse consequences, both social and physical, from their drinking.

56A4

These patients blend the styles of the Narcissist, Antisocial, and Histrionic. In addition to the traits provided in the 56A code type, these patients are even more dramatic, attention seeking, seductive, superficially affable, and gregarious. Millon theorizes that their basic conflict is between a need for constant approval, attention, and self-affirmation and a fear that people will try to control them.

Research.

1. Using cluster analysis, Mayer and Scott (1988) found this code among 28/112 (22%) male inpatient alcoholics, and Donat et al. (1992) found this code among 27/195 (14%) psychiatric inpatients.

56B

These people are Narcissistic. As such, they have an inflated sense of self-worth and are arrogant and self-reliant. They constantly seek recognition and admiration and exploit people to get it. They expect special considerations and can be socially intimidating. Millon believes that these behaviors hide a deep insecurity about their sense of self-worth, perhaps stemming from past humiliations. In addition, they are also overly touchy and prone toward aggressive and brutal acts.

Diagnosis. Consider Narcissistic Personality Disorder with aggressive or sadistic traits.

Research.

1. Craig, Verinis, and Wechsler (1985) found that this profile accounted for 31/100 opiate addicts in treatment.

2. Craig and Olson (1990) found this modal code for separate samples of cocaine (N=107) and heroin (N=86) addicts.

3. Marsh, Stile, Stoughton, and Trout-Landen (1988) found a 5,6,T code for 159 opiate addicts. They would be described as impulsive and extroverted.

57

These patients are essentially Narcissistic in personality style.

Research.

1. Lohr, Hamberger, and Bonge (1988) found this cluster in 48 spouse abusers (both scales below BR 70). They were described as narcissistic and compulsive-conforming, had no severe personality features nor any clinical symptoms, and were considered nonpathological.

576B

Two personality types may be associated with this code type. The first type shows primarily Narcissistic personality traits. They use compulsive behaviors and defenses to establish and maintain narcissistic supplies, particularly self-affirmation and attention, but may respond with vindictive anger, aggression, or brutality if these defenses do not hold. Millon theorizes that these patients fear autonomy. A second type may behave in a socially appropriate and controlled manner and demonstrate the personality traits more often associated with a Compulsive personality style. However, they remain Narcissistic and are prone to emotional outbursts.

58A

These patients show behaviors associated with the Narcissistic personality style. When they experience a narcissistic injury, they tend to respond with negativistic, oppositional, and passive-aggressive behavior and demonstrate an erratic, moody, and resentful emotionality until they get their way. Their primary goal is to acquire as much attention, praise, recognition, approval, and special considerations as they can acquire. Millon believes that unconsciously they have little self-esteem. They are prone to sexual excesses, substance abuse, and marital problems.

Diagnosis. Narcissistic Personality Disorder with passive-aggressive traits.

Scale 6 Codes

6A45

This code suggests a sociopathic or Antisocial Personality Disorder with narcissistic, self-dramatizing, and attention-seeking behaviors. (There is probably little difference between this code type and the 6A54 code type. Both can be described accurately using the 6A5 code description.)

6A5

These patients are arrogant, aggressive, self-centered, resentful, suspicious, socially intimidating, competitive, self-reliant, belligerent, touchy, jealous, vindictive, unsentimental, and inclined to brood and hold grudges. Millon theorizes that these behaviors hide deep-seated insecurities about their sense of self-worth, and are used to counteract anticipated humiliation and rejection. Their deeply felt resentment is projected outward, resulting in frequent squabbles and family arguments. They are prone to sudden and unexpected brutality. Millon also theorizes that these patients believe they must outwit others and exert power over them before they are dominated themselves. Hence they are constantly alert and vigilant to stop any perceived malice. Closeness to others is viewed as a sign of weakness and so they must act in a tough and callous manner. Overt antisocial behavior, lying, social irresponsibilities, and substance abuse are frequently seen in patients with this profile code.

Diagnosis. Antisocial Personality Disorder with narcissistic traits.

Research.

1. Lohr, Hamberger, and Bonge (1988) found this was the modal code of 74 spouse abusers. They were considered to be antisocial, aggressive, and narcissistic with some paranoid features. They used alcohol and abused drugs, and expressed anger directly. They were highly self-centered with a greatly inflated sense of importance and entitlement in marital relationships. They ordered their spouse around and expected obedience. They became abusive when their spouse failed to agree with them. Their domestic violence was not motivated to vent anger but rather as a correction measure to get their spouse to do it their way. They had little capacity for resolving conflict through traditional, nonaggressive instrumental behaviors. They externalized responsibility for their emotional reactions and for their abusive behavior.

2. This was the modal profile among a group of 119 male prison inmates who had a clinical diagnosis of psychopathy/antisocial personality disorder (Hart, Forth, & Hare, 1991).

6A54

This code describes a person who is angry, volatile, aggressive, narcissistic, unpredictable, antisocial, sullen, moody, extremely frustrated and conflicted, attention seeking, and charming and seductive, but manipulative and shallow. (There is probably little difference between this code type and the 6A45 code type. Both can be described accurately using the 6A5 code description).

Research.
1. Hamberger and Hastings (1986) found this code in 12/99 males in a domestic violence abatement program.

6A58A

These patients are quite competitive, independent, unempathic, aggressive, exploitive, defiant, hostile, narcissistic, distrustful and suspicious of others, obstructionistic, moody, negativistic, and passive-aggressive. People are viewed to be taken advantage of, and altruism is seen as a sign of weakness. They act in an arrogant, self-assured, and self-righteous manner. They are insensitive or indifferent to the rights of others. An intimidating style is also seen. When crossed, they are prone to explosive and vindictive behavior. Millon theorizes that their basic conflict is a desire to relate on a more intimate level and a fear that such response on their part will result in their being controlled and dominated, thus leading them to adopt a negativistic response pattern.

Diagnosis. Consider Antisocial Personality Disorder with narcissistic and passive-aggressive traits.

Research.
1. Corbisiero and Reznikoff (1991) found this cluster among a group of 58/247 alcoholics. They had serious and widespread problems associated with their drinking.

6A7

This pattern suggests a major conflict to behave in a rigid, tense, and conscientious manner and a tendency to vent more hostile and self-centered urges. They are assertive, self-reliant, and competitive. They feel disdain for those perceived as weak. They are disciplined, but asocial behaviors may appear. They tend to plan ahead, enjoy discipline, and control their emotions. They are very hard-working people when acting in their own self-interests.

Research.

1. Bartsch and Hoffman (1985) found that a group of 19/125 inpatient alcoholics had this code along with an MMPI 42' code. Alcohol in these patients may dampen an overly exuberant conscience, permit escape from feelings of responsibility, or permit the expression of anger.

6A8A5

These patients show behaviors that combine the features of the Antisocial, Passive-Aggressive, and Narcissistic personality styles. Traits that describe them include touchy, irascible, resentful, unpredictable, moody, negative, faultfinding, stubborn, irritable, and pessimistic, with erratic behavior and uncontrolled emotions. Millon theorizes that these patients have an intense conflict between dependency and self-assertion which leads to impulsivity and irritable moods. Though they desire closeness and intimacy, they are too untrusting and suspicious, believing that others will try to control them and hence they would become more dependent. They are constantly conflicted about acting out or controlling their resentments. Millon further believes that desires for retribution for past perceived grievances underlie their hostility and negativity. Antisocial behaviors may or may not be present, but the antisocial traits are part of their personality makeup.

Diagnosis. Mixed Personality Disorder with passive-aggressive and antisocial traits.

6B2

These people tend to be hostile, stern, judgmental, and self-righteous. They appear cold and harsh and rarely show any warmth or intimacy. Their resentments and anger can erupt into temper tantrums and emotional outbursts that can eventuate into abusive behaviors. Millon theorizes that they have been humiliated or in some way aggrieved; they behave in such ways to vindicate past hurts and, through a kind of repetition compulsion, try to overcome these hurts with other relationships. They seem to have issues with rejection, though this may be unconscious.

6B4

These patients appear sociable and friendly, but they have problems controlling their temper. Intimate acquaintances know them to be argumentative, irritable, and moody and to display self-dramatizing behaviors that may include seductiveness. Anger and badgering are used to control others. Cheerfulness can suddenly change to verbal abuse and hostility when stressed or provoked. They generally want their own way and can be insistently intimidating to get it. Depending on the kind of relationship they have with intimate others, violent and/or physically abusive behavior may ensue. Clinicians should explore the possibility of unreported spouse abuse (as perpetrators) in these patients.

6B57

These patients are characteristically edgy, jealous, and aggressive. They hold grudges and try to provoke fear in order to intimidate and control others. They are self-centered, self-reliant, and narcissistic. They believe certain rules or regulations simply do not apply to them. Their anger and resentments, suggested also by elevations on Scale 7, are often projected onto others for perceived slights.

Diagnosis. Consider Personality Disorder Not Otherwise Specified with prominent aggressive and narcissistic traits.

6B6A

This code suggests an Antisocial Personality Disorder with aggressive characteristics.

Research.

1. Male spouse abusers (*N*=49) attained this as their modal code (Beasley & Stoltenberg, 1992).

SCALE 7 CODES

723

This pattern shows combined features of compulsive and dependent behaviors. These patients are overcontrolled and defensive. They lead a restrictive, perfectionistic, and compliant life-style at the expense of spontaneous behavior and relaxation. They are vigilantly alert to avoid social transgressions that may cause them problems and the disapproval of valued authority figures.

They avoid situations that require change. They also must guard against a tendency to be argumentative, resentful, and critical of others, particularly of subordinates. They are caught between a desire to let loose and a fear that such behavior will lead to rejection and disapproval.

728A

These patients relate in a manner that is consistent with a conforming/compulsive personality style. They want others to take care of them but resent the control inherent in such relationships. The conflict between wanting dependent relationships but assiduously avoiding them occasionally erupts in negativistic behaviors, moodiness, and projected blame. Sensitivity to rejection may also be present.

73

These patients are both conforming and dependent. Salient traits include achievement strivings, intrapunitiveness, behavior rigidity, moralistic attitudes, conscientiousness, and perfectionism. They relate to others in a submissive style, which serves to protect them against criticism and against their own hostility and resentment. Their self-image is one of correctness and propriety. They identify with idealized authority figures whose values they both espouse and admire. By conforming they can secure approval and affection from others. They are usually quite efficient and organized. These patients tend to avoid criticism by presenting a superficially friendly and compliant behavior. Although they show a facile interpersonal demeanor, clinicians can expect them to be guarded and defensive concerning their personal problems. They tend to show fewer psychiatric symptoms on symptom-rating scales.

Research.

1. Levine et al. (1985) found that many patients with this code had a 27/72 MMPI code.

2. Using cluster analysis, Mayer and Scott (1988) found this code (in sub-clinical ranges) among 21/112 (17%) of male inpatient alcoholics. These patients tended to report a late onset of problematic drinking.

3. This code was found among 31/195 (16%) of psychiatric inpatients (Donat et al., 1992).

74

These patients have primarily compulsive and histrionic elements as a personality core. Both dramatic and disciplined, they are emotionally controlled, rigid, and intense, but at times they are emotionally labile. Appearance and conformity are valued, yet they try to draw attention to themselves through their perfectionistic and industrious talents and behaviors. They unconsciously desire attention and approval and fear the disapproval of those whom they are trying to impress.

Research.

1. Lemkau, Purdy, Rafferty, and Rudisill (1988) found this code among a group of 67 Family Practice residents (in subclinical ranges) reflecting a compulsive personality style.

75

Both compulsive and narcissistic elements are primarily extant in this personality configuration. They believe they are a cut above others and value their own opinions. They are self-reliant, industrious, efficient, and demanding. Inflexibility is one of their hallmarks, as they tend to believe they are always right.

76A (subclinical range)

These people are seen as cautious, proper, polite, compulsive, and retiring. They prefer stable environments and clearly defined social boundaries. They value security. They are low on exhibition and understanding and tend to be followers rather than leaders.

Research.

1. Retzlaff and Gibertini (1987) found this cluster among a group of Air Force pilot trainees in subclinical ranges.

78A

These people present as self-righteous and perfectionistic, but underneath this demeanor are hostility, harsh judgmental attitudes, and an ever-present vigilance of perceived malice. They suppress their resentments, but maintain an anger over past grievances. They value hard work and discipline and avoid displays of warmth and intimacy. They are prone to outbursts of anger and temper. They usually blame others for their problems and can become querulous, negative, faultfinding, and oppositional, particularly with people in subordinate positions.

Scale 8 Codes

Introductory Commentary on 8A Code Types

Research has established that patients with clinical elevations on Scale 8A are quite disturbed. Patients with BR scores >74 on Scale 8A should receive a thorough clinical evaluation and screening for serious psychopathology.

8A12

These patients rely on others for emotional support and security and have problems behaving independently. However, they also feel that people are undependable, unreliable, and will take advantage of them. Hence, they vacillate between behaving negativistically through passive-aggressive behaviors and acting in a compliant and agreeable manner. The personality description of the 8A126A code type is applicable to these patients, except for the antisocial features.

Research.

1. This was the modal profile for a group of white, male psychiatric patients (*N*=115) described as angry but nonpsychotic (Greenblatt & Davis, 1992).

8A126A

These patients show both Schizoid and Antisocial features amidst a primary negativistic and passive-aggressive personality style. They are mostly quiet, docile, and dependent, show deficits in social relationships, and have low self-esteem. Various behavioral eccentricities and cognitive deficits may be present. Outwardly they appear depressed and apathetic. They remain on the periphery of society, but they are also complaining, negativistic, faultfinding, stubborn, and petulant. They are mostly introverted, but significant antisocial attitudes and behaviors may coexist with their dependent and passive-aggressive personality.

Diagnosis. Schizoid/Antisocial.

8A2

The following adjectives describe patients with the 8A2 profile code: oversensitive, fearful, self-preoccupied, disgruntled, uneasy, irritable, moody, unsettled, negativistic, anxious, complaining, and powerless (Hyer, Woods, &

Boudewyns, 1991). These patients may be considered as an emotionally acting-out group, reacting to stress on an emotional level through intensely expressed affect. They tend to have temper tantrums and show explosive and angry outbursts. Anger is the affect most often expressed, but they are filled with resentments that may be acted out. They have a conflict between their dependency needs and their wish for independence. The style is conceptually close to the Borderline Personality Disorder, though less severe. If Scale C is also elevated, then emphasize Borderline traits.

Diagnosis. Passive-Aggressive Personality Disorder.

Consider Borderline Personality Disorder if Scale C is also elevated. This code may predict an unfavorable response to treatment, perhaps due to the detached, ambivalent, erratic, and provocative character style that results in chronic interpersonal problems.

Note. This profile code has been found among patients who over-report or exaggerate their symptoms.

Research.

1. This code has frequently been found as modal among inpatient male veterans with PTSD (Hyer & Boudewyns, 1985; Hyer, Woods, & Boudewyns, 1991; Hyer, Woods, Boudewyns, Harrison, & Tamkin, 1990; McDermott, 1987; Robert et al., 1985; Sherwood, Funari, & Piekarski, 1990).

2. Hyer et al. (1988) found this code among 60 inpatient PTSD male veterans. It suggests affective lability, contrary behavior, problems with self-control, isolation, low self-image, anxiety, apprehension, restlessness, and depression.

3. Hyer et al. (1989) reported that this code did not change after 35 days of residential treatment for PTSD. This code type has also appeared with some frequency in patients with substance abuse problems.

4. Cluster analysis revealed this code among N=89 alcoholics (Retzlaff & Bromley, 1991), among 65/247 alcoholics (Corbisiero & Reznikoff, 1991), and among 48/112 (38%) male inpatient alcoholics, indicating fluctuations between deference and aggressive and negativistic behavior (Mayer & Scott, 1988). These patients showed widespread characterological problems and symptomatology.

5. McMahon, Davidson, and Flynn (1986) found this code among a sample of 256 inpatient alcoholics who were high functioning.

6. McMahon and Davidson (1986) found this mean code to characterize a group of 144 inpatient alcoholics with depression.

7. Craig, Verinis, and Wexler (1985) found this pattern in 28/100 opiate addicts in treatment.

8. Joffe and Regan (1991) found this modal code among 21 patients with affective disorder whose family history was positive for depression.

9. This was the modal code among a group (N=19) of patients in a short-term psychotherapy treatment program for bulimia, who did not respond to treatment (Garner et al., 1990).

10. Antoni et al. (1985a) found that many patients with this code had a 28/82 MMPI code.

11. Repko and Cooper (1985) found this was the mean code (in subclinical ranges) for a group of Worker's Compensation claimants with psychological complaints. The personality disorder scales were generally below BR 65.

8A21

In addition to the personality characteristics described in the 8A2 pattern, the addition of the Schizoid dimension to the character style suggests that these patients are interpersonally aloof, behaviorally lethargic, cognitively impoverished, affectively flat, and relatively devoid of interpersonal skills.

Research.

1. This was the modal profile of a group of white, male psychiatric patients (N=215) described as angry and psychotic (Greenblatt & Davis, 1992).

8A213

In this code, the submissive personality style is added to the basic 8A21 character type. These patients have a poor self-image, interpersonal submission, and passivity. These traits may temper some of the negativistic behaviors seen in the 8A21 code type. Their dependence may serve to decrease complaints and symptoms but also may increase compliance to treatment.

Research.

1. This code type was found in 33/100 male patients with PTSD (Hyer, Woods, & Boudewyns, 1991).

8A216A

This is a particularly problematic character style, which, combined with the traits of the 8A21 code, is action oriented, hostile, interpersonally vindictive, and relatively fearless. Acting out is their main "defense." This pattern may decompensate, under stress, into a Paranoid condition.

Research.

1. This was the modal code among 30/100 male patients with PTSD (Hyer, Woods, & Boudewyns, 1991).

8A23

These patients are moody and resentful, but their hostility is usually expressed in passive-aggressive behaviors. They feel insecure, lonely, and uncomfortable in social relationships. They show irritability and substantial variation in mood, but are dependent and sensitive to rejection. With their angry emotions and faultfinding behavior they may elicit the rejection they anticipate.

Research.

1. Bartsch and Hoffman (1985) found this code in 35/123 inpatient alcoholics. They theorized that drinking may serve a self-medication function for this group. Because of their personality features of ambivalence and negativism, they may have great difficulty following through with aftercare. Their avoidant and suspicious qualities suggest that they may also be reluctant to purse AA. Their MMPI profile code was 84127'.

2. McMahon, Davidson, and Flynn (1986) found a similar code among a sample of 256 inpatient, lower-social-functioning alcoholics. These patients were socially detached and isolated, dysphoric, and felt misunderstood and unappreciated. They showed more personality disturbance, greater debilitating clinical symptoms, and fewer adaptive personality traits than higher functioning alcoholics.

3. This was the modal code of alcoholics (N=256 white males; McMahon, Gersh, & Davidson, 1989) and inpatient alcoholics (N=125) who were continuous drinkers (McMahon, Davidson, Gersh, & Flynn, 1991).

4. Joffe and Regan (1988) found this code among 42 patients with Major Depression. This code disappeared in the remitted state.

5. Depressed patients who responded to tricyclic antidepressants (N=23/42) had this as a modal code (Joffe & Regan, 1989a). The code disappeared in the remitted state, where the MCMI profile was a subclinical Spike 7' code.

6. Libb et al. (1990) found this code among 28 patients with Major Depression (outpatients). This code is disappeared in the remitted state, where the MCMI profile showed a 3' code.

7. This was the modal code for *N*=27 Borderlines (Lewis & Harder, 1991).

8. This was the modal code (with Scale C also elevated) among a group of 10 suicide attempters (Joffe & Regan, 1989b).

8A26A

This code combines the personality trait elements of passive-aggressive, avoidant, and antisocial. Refer to the 8A2 code type description and then add antisocial traits for additional description.

Diagnosis. Consider Borderline Personality Disorder with passive-aggressive traits.

8A3

Millon's theory classifies these patients as ambivalently dependent. He considers their cardinal feature to be a struggle between independence and assertion on the one hand and submissive dependency and security on the other. This results in unstable emotions, interpersonal conflicts, and impulsive and acting-out behavior. They may enter into a symbiotic-like relationship to an overvalued and idealized person whom the patient hopes will satisfy their dependency needs. Eventually they come to view this person in a negative and rejecting manner, resulting in depression or angry outbursts. Millon theorizes that a decompensation appears to follow a borderline pattern.

Research.

1. Research has reported that patients with this modal profile had MMPI codes consisting of 89/98 (Antoni et al., 1986), 27/72 (Levine et al., 1985), or 24/42 (Antoni et al., 1985b).

2. Stark and Campbell (1988) found this code to be characteristic of a group of drug abusers who completed a treatment program.

8A32

In addition to the personality description provided in the 8A3 code type, these patients are submissive and dependent. They assume a passive and clinging role in relationships. If the BR score on Scale 8A is BR<75, then it may reflect social introversion, confusion, and withdrawal, but not psychosis. In this case the symptom picture is probably dominated by anxiety and depression. If Scale 8A has a BR score of >75, then the traits inherent to the Passive-Aggressive scale should be stressed instead of the dependent features associated with the 32 code type.

Diagnosis. Consider Mixed Personality Disorder with dependent and passive-aggressive traits, or Borderline Personality Disorder.

Research.

1. Hamberger and Hastings (1986) found this code among 14/99 males in a domestic violence abatement program. These patients were considered to be sullen, moody, and avoidant, with intense dependency conflicts. They showed pronounced mood swings, and psychotic tendencies may have appeared.

2. Wetzler, Kahn, Strauman, and Dubro (1989) found this code as modal among a sample of 48 patients with Major Depression. This reflects an absence of self-esteem, emotional lability, an ambivalent dependency with indirect expressions of anger, extreme sensitivity to signs of rejection, and a tendency to pull away from social contact in anticipation of rejection.

3. Cluster analysis found this code among a group of (N=89) alcoholics (Retzlaff & Bromley, 1991).

4. Snibbe, Peterson, and Sosner (1980) found that this mean profile was characteristic of a psychiatric "stress & strain" (N=11) group, and low back pain (N=6) for Worker's Compensation claimants.

8A321

These patients are passive-aggressive and avoidant with borderline and paranoid features. They are anxious, dysthymic, may abuse drugs and alcohol, and may express anger directly. They demand approval and absolute loyalty from a spouse. These patients fear losing the respect of their spouse and their own self-respect. They may have a Borderline Personality Disorder, lack inner resources for maintaining self-esteem, and develop intense symbiotic relationships that are highly conflictual and emotionally volatile.

Research.

1. Using cluster analysis, Lohr, Hamberger, and Bonge (1988) found this code among 66 male spouse abusers.

8A345

Research.

1. Hamberger and Hastings (1986) found this code among 11/99 males in a domestic violence abatement program. They show anxious bids for support and fear separation and loss. They alternate between periods of moodiness, futility, and dejection and occasional impulsive angry outbursts.

8A4

These patients have deficits in primary emotional expression. They have continued interpersonal squabbles and arguments due to their testy behaviors. They tend to sulk or become moody at one time and then react in a friendly, congenial, and dramatic way in order to get attention. They become angry, negativistic, and hostile when they don't get their way. They are prone to suicidal gestures and/or substance abuse.

Diagnosis. Passive-Aggressive personality with histrionic traits.

Research.

1. Cluster analysis found this code for $N=44/150$ alcoholics (Donat, 1988; Donat, Walters, & Hume, 1991).

2. This was the modal profile among a group of outpatients ($N=15$) with a diagnosis of Panic Disorder (Reich, 1990).

8A42

These patients react to stress with labile, angry affect and extreme moodiness. Behind a negative and histrionic response style is a sensitivity to rejection. Millon theorizes that their essential style features a deep ambivalence and hostility generated by conflict between a desire for dependence and a wish for independence. This results in continuous emotional displays and histrionic behaviors.

Research.

1. Antoni et al. (1987) found that many patients with this MCMI code had an MMPI 78/87 code.

8A54

Research.

1. This was the modal profile among a group of (*N*=14) patients with a diagnosis of Major Depression (Wetzler, Kahn, Cahn, van Praag, & Asnis, 1990).

8A56A

These patients have difficulty controlling anger, given their confident and competitive personality style. They are moody, irritable, and resentful when frustrated. They may act out overtly or express their resentment in passive-aggressive behaviors. They feel they are a special person and should be treated accordingly, and they can become enraged when others do not treat them in an "appropriate" manner. They are prone to antisocial behavior and legal problems. Millon believes that underneath this overt behavior are severe dependency needs that require satisfaction.

8A6A

These patients are both negativistic and antisocial. They are conflicted, moody, irritable, resentful, unempathic and uncaring, self-centered, sullen, have a low tolerance for frustration, and tend to act out. If there is no antisocial behavior in their history, then the Passive-Aggressive style should be emphasized; if antisocial behavior is present, then the Antisocial style should be emphasized.

Diagnosis. R/o Passive-Aggressive Personality Disorder with antisocial traits, or r/o Antisocial Personality Disorder with passive-aggressive traits.

8A6A2

In addition to the personality description reported for the 8A6A code type, these patients also have significant avoidant features, tend to be vigilantly alert to perceived acts of derogation, and are characteristically angry and hostile.

Diagnosis. Borderline with passive-aggressive and antisocial traits.

Research.

1. Hamberger and Hastings (1986) found this code in 10/99 men in a domestic violence abatement program. These patients were described as withdrawn, moody, asocial, and overly sensitive to interpersonal slights. They were highly volatile and overreacted to trivial matters. They were calm and controlled one moment and extremely angry and oppressive the

next moment. They had high levels of anxiety and depression, and this personality style made them prone to anger. Their DSM-III diagnosis suggested Borderline Personality Disorder.

8A6A4

These patients demonstrate a mixture of negativistic, competitive, and dramatic traits, erratic moods, anger, resentment, and obstructionistic behaviors. They have prominent antisocial personality traits and strive to maintain their independence and avoid being controlled.

8A6B

This code suggests serious emotional maladjustment. These patients are negativistic, behaviorally erratic, pessimistic, temperamental, and unpredictable. In addition to their underlying anger and resentment, they have a potential for assaultive behavior. Their interpersonal life is filled with conflict due to their uncooperative behavior and belligerent threats.

8A6B6A

The behavior of these people is similar to that described in the 8A6B code, except that antisocial traits are further integrated into their personality.

8A71

These patients show the traits described in the passive-aggressive (negativistic) character type. However, they try to control their petulance and acting-out propensities through rigid and compulsive behaviors. These patients tend to be seriously disturbed, are prone to act out in vicious ways, either against themselves or at others, and should be closely examined and perhaps hospitalized, if warranted.

Research.

1. This was the modal profile of black, male psychiatric patients (N=105) described as angry and psychotic (Greenblatt & Davis, 1992).

8A8B2

This profile code suggests people who are negativistic, embittered, resentful, moody, faultfinding, petulant, pessimistic, angry, and stubborn. They are prone to impulsive outbursts. In addition, they permit themselves to be exploited and abused, and tend to sabotage the good that people try to do for them, presenting a picture of a person who has suffered throughout life. With their many complaints and manifestations of self-pity, they tend to demoralize those around them, who lose patience with their obstructionistic behavior. Behind these personality manifestations are deeply dependent individuals who are conflicted between self-assertion and their need for dependency.

Research.

1. This was the modal code of 26 psychiatric inpatients diagnosed with Borderline Personality Disorder (McCann, Flynn, & Gersh, 1992).

2. This code was found among 35/195 (18%) psychiatric inpatients (Donat et al., 1992). They showed intense interpersonal ambivalence, extreme sensitivity to criticism, and frequently misinterpreted the behavior of others as critical. They acted in a negativistic and discontented fashion. They also showed high levels of psychiatric symptoms.

8A6A6B5

Research.

1. This was the modal profile for a subgroup of patients described as antisocial-aggressive/sadistic and passive/aggressive (Lohr & Strack, 1990).

8B23

Research.

1. This was the pretreatment modal profile of 43 outpatients prior to beginning pharmacological treatment for Major Depression (Stankovic, Libb, Freeman, & Roseman, 1992).

8B28A

Research.

1. This was the modal code for a group (N=11) of patients with the diagnosis of Borderline Personality Disorder (Fink & Golinkoff, 1990).

8B6A4

These patients are constantly edgy, unpredictable, sullenly angry, and chronically bitter. Thus, they have the potential to become suddenly aggressive, assaultive, and explosively angry and brutal. They are negativistic, stubborn, uncooperative, and antagonistic. They carry a chip-on-the-shoulder attitude and are often belligerent. These behaviors are often controlled through passive-aggressive behaviors. Expect self-dramatizing and approval-seeking behaviors during periods of calmness.

Diagnosis. Consider Passive Aggressive Personality Disorder with aggressive traits, or Personality Disorder Not Otherwise Specified with prominent aggressive and passive-aggressive traits.

8B8A2

These patients use passive-aggressive and avoidant defenses to control their aggression, but have trouble doing so. They are sensitive to perceived criticism, and, combined with a touchy irritability, they are prone to act out their anger on the nearest target.

Research.

1. This was the modal profile of patients described as avoidant-schizoid and self-defeating (Lohr & Strack, 1990).

Diagnosis. Consider Passive Aggressive Personality Disorder with aggressive traits, or Personality Disorder Not Otherwise Specified with prominent aggressive and passive-aggressive traits.

MISCELLANEOUS CODES

CADH (***Note.*** No personality disorder scales were clinically elevated.)

Research.

1. Repko and Cooper (1985) found this pattern as the mean configuration among 100 Worker's Compensation claimants. Most of the personality disorder scales were below 65.

Adams, W. E., & Clopton, J. R. (1990). Personality and dissonance among Mormon missionaries. *Journal of Personality Assessment, 54,* 684-693.

Antoni, M., (1993). The combined use of the MCMI and MMPI. In. R. J. Craig (Ed.). *The Millon Clinical Multiaxial Inventory: A clinical research information synthesis* (pp. 279-302). Hillsdale, NJ: Lawrence Erlbaum.

Antoni, M., Levine, J., Tischer, P., Green, C., & Millon, T. (1986). Refining personality assessments by combining MCMI high-point profiles and MMPI codes, part IV: MMPI Code 89/98. *Journal of Personality Assessment, 50,* 65-72.

Antoni, M., Levine, J., Tischer, P., Green, C., & Millon, T. (1987). Refining personality assessments by combining MCMI high-point profiles and MMPI codes, part V: MMPI Code 78/87. *Journal of Personality Assessment, 51,* 375-387.

Antoni, M., Tischer, P., Levine, J., Green, C., & Millon, T. (1985a). Refining personality assessments by combining MCMI high-point profiles and MMPI codes, part I: MMPI Code 28/82. *Journal of Personality Assessment, 49,* 392-398.

Antoni, M., Tischer, P., Levine, J., Green, C., & Millon, T. (1985b). Refining personality assessments by combining MCMI high-point profiles and MMPI codes, part III: MMPI Code 24/42. *Journal of Personality Assessment, 49,* 508-515.

Bagby, R. M., Gillis, J. R., & Rogers, R. (1991). Effectiveness of the Millon Clinical Multiaxial Inventory Validity Index in the detection of random responding. *Psychology Assessment, 3,* 185-287.

Bartsch, T. & Hoffman, J. (1985). A cluster analysis of Millon Clinical Multiaxial Inventory (MCMI) profiles: More about a taxonomy of alcoholic subtypes. *Journal of Clinical Psychology, 41,* 707-713.

Beasley, R., & Stoltenberg, C. D. (1992). Personality characteristics of male spouse abusers. *Professional Psychology: Research and Practice, 23,* 310-317.

Bryer, J. B., Nelson, B. A., Miller, J. B., & Krol, P. A. (1987). Childhood sexual and physical abuse as factors in adult psychiatric illness. *American Journal of Psychiatry, 144,* 1426-1430.

Corbisiero, J. R., & Reznikoff, M. (1991). The relationship between personality type and style of alcohol use. *Journal of Personality Assessment, 47,* 291-298.

Costa, P. T., & McCrae, R. R. (1990). Personality disorders and the five-factor model of personality. *Journal of Personality Disorders, 4,* 362-371.

Craig, R. J. (Ed.). (1993). *Millon Clinical Multiaxial Inventory: A clinical and research information synthesis.* Hillsdale, NJ: Lawrence Erlbaum.

Craig, R. J., & Olson, R. E. (1990). MCMI comparisons of cocaine abusers and heroin addicts. *Journal of Clinical Psychology, 46,* 230-237.

Craig, R. J., Verinis, J. S., & Wexler, S. (1985). Personality characteristics of drug addicts and alcoholics on the Millon Clinical Multiaxial Inventory. *Journal of Personality Assessment, 49,* 156-160.

Craig, R. J., & Weinberg, D. (1992a). Assessing alcoholics with the Millon Clinical Multiaxial Inventory: A review. *Psychology of Addictive Behaviors, 6,* 200-208.

Craig, R. J., & Weinberg, D. (1992b). Assessing drug abusers with the Millon Clinical Multiaxial Inventory: A review. *Journal of Substance Abuse Treatment, 9,* 1-7.

Donat, D. C. (1988). Millon Clinical Multiaxial Inventory (MCMI) clusters for alcohol abusers: Further evidence for validity and implications for medical psychotherapy. *Medical Psychotherapy, 1,* 41-50.

Donat, D. C., Geczy, B., Helmrich, J., & LeMay, M. (1992). Empirically derived personality subtypes of public psychiatric patients: Effect of self-reported symptoms, coping inclinations, and evaluation of expressed emotion in caregivers. *Journal of Personality Assessment, 58,* 36-50.

Donat, D. C., Walters, J., & Hume, A. (1991). Personality characteristics of alcohol dependent inpatients: Relationship of MCMI subtypes to self-reported drinking behavior. *Journal of Personality Assessment, 57,* 335-344.

Fals-Stewart, W. (1992). Personality characteristics of substance abusers: An MCMI cluster typology of recreational drug users treated in a therapeutic community and its relationship to length of stay and outcome. *Journal of Personality Assessment, 59,* 515-527.

Fink, D., & Golinkoff, D. (1990). MPD, borderline personality disorder and schizophrenia: A comparative study of clinical features. *Dissociation, 8,* 127-134.

Garner, D. M., Olmsted, M. P., Davis, R., Rockert, W., Goldbloom, D., & Eagle, M. (1990). The association between bulimic symptoms and reported psychopathology. *International Journal of Eating Disorders, 9,* 1-15.

Goldberg, J. O., Segal, Z. V., Vella, D. D., & Shaw, B. F. (1989). Depressive personality: Millon Clinical Multiaxial Inventory profiles of sociotropic and autonomous subtypes. *Journal of Personality Disorders, 3,* 193-198.

Greenblatt, R. L., & Davis, W. E. (1992). Accuracy of MCMI classification of angry and psychotic black and white patients. *Journal of Clinical Psychology, 48,* 59-63.

Hamberger, L. K., & Hastings, J. E. (1986). Personality correlates of men who abuse their partners: A cross-validational study. *Journal of Family Violence, 1,* 323-341.

Hart, S. D., Forth, A. E., & Hare, R. D. (1991). The MCMI-II and psychopathy. *Journal of Personality Disorders, 5,* 318-327.

Herron, L., Turner, J., & Weiner, P. (1986). A comparison of the Millon Clinical Multiaxial Inventory and the Minnesota Multiphasic Personality Inventory as predictors of successful treatment by lumbar laminectomy. *Clinical Orthopaedics and Related Research, 203,* 232-238.

Hibbard, S. (1989). Personality and object relational pathology in young adult children of alcoholics. *Psychotherapy, 26,* 504-509.

Hyer, L., Woods, M. G., Boudewyns, P. A. (1991). A three tier evaluation of PTSD among Vietnam combat veterans. *Journal of Traumatic Stress, 4,* 165-194.

Hyer, L., Woods, M. G., Boudewyns, P. A., Bruno, R., & O'Leary, W. C. (1988). Concurrent validation of the Millon Clinical Multiaxial Inventory among Vietnam veterans with Posttraumatic Stress Disorder. *Psychological Reports, 63,* 271-278.

Hyer, L., Woods, M. G., Boudewyns, P. A., Harrison, W. R., & Tamkin, A. S. (1990). MCMI and 16PF with Vietnam veterans: Profiles and concurrent validation of MCMI. *Journal of Personality Disorders, 4,* 391-401.

Hyer, L., Woods, M. G., Bruno, R., & Boudewyns, P.A. (1989). Treatment outcomes of Vietnam veterans with PTSD and the consistency of the MCMI. *Journal of Clinical Psychology, 45,* 547-552.

Hyer, L. (1985). The 8-2 MCMI Personality Profile among Vietnam veterans with PTSD. *PTSD Newsletter, 4,* p. 2.

Jackson, J. L., Greenblatt, R. L., Davis, W. E., Murphy, T. J., & Trimkus, K. (1991). Assessment of schizophrenic inpatients with the MCMI. *Journal of Clinical Psychology, 47,* 505-510.

Jay, G. W., Grove, R. N., & Grove, K. S. (1987). Differentiation of chronic headache from non-headache pain patients using the Millon Clinical Multiaxial Inventory (MCMI). *Headache, 27,* 124-129.

Joffe, R. T., & Regan, J. J. (1988). Personality and depression. *Journal of Psychiatric Research, 22,* 279-286.

Joffe, R. T., & Regan, J. J. (1989a). Personality and response to tricyclic antidepressants in depressed patients. *Journal of Nervous and Mental Disease, 177,* 745-749.

Joffe, R. T., & Regan, J. J. (1989b). Personality and suicidal behavior in depressed patients. *Comprehensive Psychiatry, 30,* 157-160.

Joffe, R. T., & Regan, J. J. (1991). Personality and family history of depression in patients with affective illness. *Journal of Psychiatric Research, 25,* 67-71.

Joffe, R. T., Swinson, R. P., & Regan, J. J. (1988). Personality features of obsessive-compulsive disorder. *American Journal of Psychiatry, 145,* 1127-1129.

Josiassen, R. C., Shagass, C., & Roemer, R. A. (1988). Somatosensory evoked potential correlates of schizophrenic subtypes identified by Millon Clinical Multiaxial Inventory. *Psychiatry Research, 23,* 209-219.

Kennedy, S. H., McVey, G., & Katz, R. (1990). Personality disorders in anorexia nervosa and bulimia nervosa. *Journal of Psychiatric Research, 24,* 259-269.

Langevin, R., Lane, R., Reynolds, R., Wright, P., Garrew, D., Marchese, V., Handy, L., Pugh, G., & Frenzel, R. (1988). Personality and sexual anomalies: An examination of the Millon Clinical Multiaxial Inventory. *Annals of Sex Research, 1,* 13-32.

Lees-Haley, P. R. (1992). Efficacy of MMPI-2 validity scales and MCMI-II modifier scales for detecting spurious PTSD claims: F, F-K, Faked Bad Scale, Ego Strength, Subtle-Obvious subscales, DIS, and DEB. *Journal of Clinical Psychology, 48,* 681-689.

Lemkau, J. P., Purdy, R. R., Rafferty, J. P., & Rudisill, J. R. (1988). Correlates of burnout among family practice residents. *Journal of Medical Education, 63,* 682-691.

Levine, J. B., Tischer, P., Antoni, M., Green, C., & Millon, T. (1985). Refining personality assessments by combining MCMI high-point profiles and MMPI codes, part II: MMPI Code 27/72. *Journal of Personality Assessment, 49,* 501-507.

Lewis, S. J., & Harder, D. W. (1991). A comparison of four measures to diagnose DSM-III-R borderline personality disorder in outpatients. *Journal of Nervous and Mental Disease, 179,* 329-337.

Libb, J. W., Stankovic, S., Freeman, A., Sokol, R., Switzer, P., & Houck, C. (1990). Personality disorders among depressed outpatients as identified by the MCMI. *Journal of Clinical Psychology, 46,* 277-284.

Libb, J. W., Stankovic, S., Sokol, R., Freeman, A., Houck, C., & Switzer, P. (1990). Stability of the MCMI among depressed psychiatric outpatients. *Journal of Personality Assessment, 63,* 209-218.

Lohr, J. M., Hamberger, L. K., & Bonge, D. (1988). The nature of irrational beliefs in different personality clusters of spouse abusers. *Journal of Rational-Emotive and Cognitive Behavior Therapy, 6,* 273-285.

Lohr, J. M. & Strack, S. (1990). Profile clusters of the MCMI-II personality disorder scales. *Journal of Clinical Psychology, 46,* 606-612.

Mannis, M. J., Morrison, T. L., Zadnik, K., Holland, E. J., & Krachmer, J. H. (1987). Personality trends in Keratoconus. *American Journal of Ophthalmology, 101,* 798-800.

Marsh, D. T., Stile, S. A., Stoughton, N. L., & Trout-Landen, B. L. (1988). Psychopathology of opiate addiction: Comparative data from the MMPI and MCMI. *American Journal of Drug and Alcohol Abuse, 14,* 17-27.

Mayer, G. S., & Scott, K. J. (1988). An exploration of heterogeneity in an inpatient male alcoholic population. *Journal of Personality Disorders, 2,* 243-255.

McCann, J. T. (1992). A comparison of two measures for obsessive-compulsive personality disorder. *Journal of Personality Disorders, 6,* 18-23.

McCann, J. T., Flynn, P. M., & Gersh, D. M. (1992). MCMI-II diagnosis of borderline personality disorder: Base rates versus prototype items. *Journal of Personality Assessment, 58,* 105-114.

McCann, J., & Gergelis, R. E. (1990). Utility of the MCMI-II in assessing suicide risk. *Journal of Clinical Psychology, 46,* 764-770.

McCann, J., & Suess, J. (1988). Clinical application of the MCMI: The 1-2-3-8 codetype. *Journal of Clinical Psychology, 44,* 181-191.

McDermott, W. F. (1987). The diagnosis of post-traumatic stress disorder using the Millon Clinical Multiaxial Inventory. In C. Green (Ed.). *Conference on the Millon Clinical Inventories (MCMI, MBHI, MAPI)* (pp. 257-262). Minneapolis: National Computer Systems.

McMahon, R., & Davidson, R. S. (1985). Transient versus enduring depression among alcoholics in inpatient treatment. *Journal of Psychopathology and Behavioral Assessment, 7,* 317-328.

McMahon, R., & Davidson, R. S . (1986). An examination of depressed and nondepressed alcoholics in inpatient treatment. *Journal of Clinical Psychology, 42,* 177-184.

McMahon, R., & Davidson, R. S., Gersh, D., & Flynn, P. M. (1991). A comparison of continuous and episodic drinkers using the MCMI, MMPI, and ALCEVAL-R. *Journal of Clinical Psychology, 47,* 21-31.

McMahon, R., & Davidson, R. S., & Flynn, P. M. (1986). Psychological correlates and treatment outcomes for high and low social functioning alcoholics. *International Journal of the Addictions, 21,* 819-835.

McMahon, R., Gersh, D., & Davidson, R. S. (1989). Personality and symptom characteristics of continuous vs. episodic drinkers. *Journal of Clinical Psychology, 45,* 161-168.

McMahon, R., & Tyson, D. (1990). Personality factors in transient versus enduring depression among inpatient alcoholic women: A preliminary analysis. *Journal of Personality Disorders, 4,* 150-160.

McNeil, K., & Meyer, R. C. (1990). Detection of deception on the Millon Clinical Multiaxial Inventory (MCMI). *Journal of Clinical Psychology, 46,* 755-764.

Millon, T. (1983). *Millon Clinical Multiaxial Inventory Manual.* Minneapolis: National Computer Systems.

Millon, T. (1984). Interpretive guide to the Millon Clinical Multiaxial Inventory. In P. McReynolds and G. J. Chelune (Eds.). *Advances in psychological assessment. Vol. 6* (pp. 1-40). San Francisco: Jossey-Bass.

Millon, T. (1989) *Manual for the MCMI-II (2nd ed.).* Minneapolis: National Computer Systems.

Millon, T., & Green, C. (1989). Interpretive guide to the Millon Clinical Multiaxial Inventory (MCMI-II). In C. S. Newmark (Ed.), *Major psychological assessment instruments: Volume II* (pp. 5-43). Boston: Allyn and Bacon.

Murphy, T. J., Greenblatt, R. L., Mozdzierz, G. J., & Trimakas, K. A. (1990). Stability of the Millon Clinical Multiaxial Inventory among psychiatric inpatients. *Journal of Psychopathology and Behavioral Assessment, 12,* 143-150.

Ownby, R. L., Wallbrown, F. H., Carmin, C., & Barnett, R. (1991). A canonical analysis of the Millon Clinical Multiaxial Inventory and the MMPI for an offender population. *Journal of Personality Disorders, 5,* 15-24.

Piersma, H. L. (1986). The Millon Clinical Multiaxial Inventory (MCMI) as a treatment outcome measure for psychiatric inpatients. *Journal of Clinical Psychology, 42,* 493-499.

Piersma, H. L. (1987). The use of the Millon Clinical Multiaxial Inventory in the evaluation of seminary students. *Journal of Psychology and Theology, 15,* 227-233.

Repko, G. R., & Cooper, R. (1985). The diagnosis of personality disorder: A comparison of MMPI profile, Millon inventory, and clinical judgment in a Worker's Compensation population. *Journal of Clinical Psychology, 41,* 867-881.

Reich, J. (1990). The effect of personality on placebo response in panic patients. *Journal of Nervous and Mental Disease, 178,* 699-702.

Retzlaff, P. D., & Bromley, S. (1991). A multi-test alcoholic taxonomy: Canonical coefficient clusters. *Journal of Clinical Psychology, 47,* 299-309.

Retzlaff, P. D., & Gibertini, M. (1987). Air Force pilot personality: Hard data on "The right stuff." *Multivariate Behavioral Research, 22,* 383-399.

Retzlaff, P. D., & Gibertini, M. (1988, July). Objective psychological testing of U.S. Air Force officers in pilot training. *Aviation, Space, and Environmental Medicine,* pp. 661-663.

Retzlaff, P. D., & Gibertini, M. (1990). Active-duty and veteran alcoholics: Differences in psychopathology presentation. *Military Medicine, 155,* 334-336.

Retzlaff, P., Sheehan, E., & Fiel, A. (1991). MCMI-II report style and bias: Profile and validity scale analysis. *Journal of Personality Assessment, 56,* 466-477.

Robert, J. A., Ryan, J. J., McEntyre, W. L., McFarland, R. S., Lips, O., & Rosenberg, S. J. (1985). MCMI characteristics of DSM-III posttraumatic stress disorder in Vietnam veterans. *Journal of Personality Assessment, 49,* 226-230.

Sherwood, R. J., Funari, D. J., & Piekarski, A. M. (1990). Adapted character styles of Vietnam veterans with posttraumatic stress disorder. *Psychological Reports, 66,* 623-631.

Snibbe, J. R., Peterson, P. J., & Sosner, B. (1980). Study of psychological characteristics of a Worker's Compensation sample using the MMPI and the Millon Clinical Multiaxial Inventory. *Psychological Reports, 47,* 959-966.

Stankovic, S. R., Libb, J. W., Freeman, A. M., & Roseman, J. M. (1992). Posttreatment stability of the MCMI-II personality scales in depressed outpatients. *Journal of Personality Disorders, 6,* 82-89.

Stark, M. J., & Campbell, B. K. (1988). Personality, drug use, and early attrition from substance abuse treatment. *American Journal of Drug and Alcohol Abuse, 14,* 475-485.

Tango, R. A., & Dziuban, C. D. (1984). The use of personality components in the interpretation of career indecision. *Journal of College Student Personnel, 25,* 509-512.

Tisdale, M. J., Pendleton, L., & Marler, M. (1990). MCMI characteristics of DSM-III-R bulimics. *Journal of Personality Assessment, 55,* 477-483.

Wall, T. L., Schuckit, M. A., Mungas, D., & Ehlers, C. L. (1990). EEG alpha activity and personality traits. *Alcohol, 7,* 461-464.

Wetzler, S., Kahn, R., Cahn, W., van Praag, H., & Asnis, G. M. (1990). Psychological test characteristics of depressed and panic patients. *Psychiatry Research, 31,* 179-192.

Wetzler, S., Kahn, R., Strauman, T. J., & Dubro, A. (1989). Diagnosis of major depression by self-report. *Journal of Personality Assessment, 53,* 22-30.

Wetzler, S., & Marlowe, D. (1990). "Faking bad" on MMPI, MMPI-2, and Millon-II. *Psychological Reports, 67,* 1117-1118.

Wolberg, W. H., Tanner, M. A., Romsaas, E. P., Trump, D. L., & Malec, J. F. (1987). Factors influencing options in primary breast cancer treatment. *Journal of Clinical Oncology, 5,* 68-74.

Yeager, R. J., DiGuiseppe, R., Resweber, P. J., & Leaf, R. (1992). Comparison of Millon personality profiles of chronic residential substance abusers and a general outpatient population. *Psychological Reports, 71,* 71-79.

5. INTEGRATING THE MCMI-II INTO AN OBJECTIVE TEST BATTERY

Multiaxial diagnosis, as conceived and presented in DSM-III-R, requires a clinical diagnostic evaluation of both psychopathology, as manifested by specific clinical syndromes (Axis I), and personality disorders (Axis II) that may affect the course and duration of the clinical syndrome. Most objective personality tests, such as the MMPI-2, have historically provided clinicians with excellent descriptive information about a wide range of personality variables and symptom clusters that are relevant in understanding behavior, but they are less specific in the determination of DSM-III-R-related diagnostic categories. MMPI-2 code types have not been isomorphically specific to diagnostic categories, except in a very broad way, such as the 123' code type associated with Somatoform Disorder, and the 49' code type associated with Antisocial Personality Disorder. Attempts to develop personality disorder scales from the MMPI item pool (Morey, Waugh, & Blashfield, 1985) have generated little empirical research, to date, and are not routinely scored in most computer-narrative programs.

The Millon Clinical Multiaxial Inventory-(II) is an objective test of personality that provides information on both clinical syndromes and personality styles and/or disorders. The inclusion and integration of the MCMI-II with other objective personality tests into an "Objective Personality Test Battery" may provide data in different domains of psychological functioning, or could provide internal corroboration of clinical interpretations. The combination of multiple assessment instruments, using projective tests such as the Rorschach, TAT, and Figure Drawings, is common clinical practice, yet there has been little presentation in the published literature on using a similar kind of approach with objective personality tests.

This chapter will present a literature review on integrating the MCMI-II into an objective test battery, and then demonstrate, at the clinical level, the combined use of the MCMI-II with other objective personality tests using the case example approach. I will attempt to show how the combined use of these two instruments can synergize, refine, and individualize personality assessment and interpretation. Examples will be provided which demonstrate the unique value that each test brings to the assessment process, and how consensual validity can be obtained through their combined use.

Literature Review

As noted earlier, there has been little attention in the literature on combining objective personality tests into an objective test battery. Michael Antoni and his group at the University of Miami at Coral Gables (where Ted Millon is also based) have done the most work on this topic (Antoni, 1992; Antoni, Levine, Tischer, Green, & Millon, 1985a, 1985b, 1986, 1987; Levine, Antoni, Tischer, Green, & Millon, 1985; Levine, Tischer, Antoni, Green, & Millon, 1985). The methodology for their research has been essentially the same for each of their several papers. First, 175 clinicians from across the country submitted a total of 3283 sets of MCMI and MMPI test protocols. Second, from this pool they identified patients with common MMPI code types, and the MCMI code types were tallied. The sample sizes from the published data were rather substantial. For MMPI code type 28/82, the sample consisted of 353 sets of MCMIs and MMPIs; for code type 24/42, there were 318 sets; for the 49/94 code type, 305 sets; for the 78/87, 272 sets; for the 98/89, 228 sets; for the 27/72, 228 sets; and for the 48/84, the total sample consisted of 202 sets of tests. This work is more thoroughly presented by Antoni (1993) and only briefly will be presented here.

For MMPI code type 42/24, the researchers found an Interpersonally Acting Out type, represented by MCMI codes 5, 6A, 6A5, and 6A7; an Interpersonally Acting In type with MCMI codes of 1, 13-8; and an Emotionally Acting Out type, associated with MCMI codes 34/43, 8A3, and 8A4.

For MMPI code type 27/72, they identified a Fearful, Dependent, Anxious type with MCMI codes of 21, 12, 21S, and 23S; a Conforming, Dependent, Anxious type, with a 73 MCMI code type; and a Dependent but Ambivalent type with MCMI codes of 8A and 8A3.

For MMPI 28/82, they found an Interpersonally Acting In type with MCMI codes of 1, 2, and 21; an Emotionally Acting Out type with MCMI codes 8A, 8A2, and 28A; and an Emotionally Acting In type, with MCMI codes 23 and 32.

For the 48/84 MMPI code type, they found an Emotional, Ambivalent type with an MCMI code of 8AC, an Emotionally Acting Out type with an MCMI code of 6A, and an Emotional, Internalizing type with MCMI codes of 23 and 32.

For the MMPI code 78/87, they found an Interpersonally Acting In type associated with MCMI codes of 12 and 21; an Emotionally Acting Out type with MCMI codes of 28A, 8A2, 8A3, and 8A4; and an Emotionally Acting In type with MCMI codes of 23 and 32.

Finally, for MMPI code 89/98, they reported an Interpersonally Acting Out type with MCMI codes of 6A5, 56A, 6A, 6A1, and 6A7; an Interpersonally Grandiose type with an MCMI code of 5; and an Emotionally Acting Out type with MCMI codes of 8A5, 8A6, 35, 34, 43, and 8A3.

Antoni's research has been the most thorough and systematic attempt to derive MCMI subtypes from MMPI code types and forms the basis of an empirical approach toward the integration of the MCMI-II with the MMPI-2 for more refined personality assessment.

The MCMI has also been combined with the 16 Personality Factors (16PF) test with Vietnam veterans (N=60) with PTSD (Hyer, Woods, Boudewyns, Harrison, & Tamkin, 1990). The MCMI-II profiles of these patients were significantly elevated on Passive-Aggressive and Avoidant (8A2), a finding that replicated past research with PTSD patients. Their 16PF profiles showed low Sten scores on Emotional Stability (Factor C), Happy-Go-Lucky (F), Boldness (H), Self-Discipline (Q3), and Extraversion, and elevated Sten scores on Insecurity (O), Self-Sufficiency (Q2), Tension (Q4), and Anxiety, reflecting a pattern of chronic tension, avoidance, fear, low self-efficacy, suspiciousness, and a general state of unhappiness.

The remaining report in the literature is a clinically based presentation. Benjamin (1987) reported on the combined use of the MCMI with the Structural Analysis of Social Behavior (SASB) (Benjamin, 1974, 1984). This procedure operationalizes patient perceptions of interpersonal experiences which were likely to have been central to the development of a personality disorder, and quantifies perceptions of important people in the patient's past and present. A computer program is available (INTREX) that "maps" specific relationships. Using the relationship concepts of opposition, similarity, and complementarity and the interpersonal processes of action, reaction, and introjection, arranged in a circumplex order, the computer-generated report allows a clinician to make a number of inferences about antecedent interpersonal experiences and about probable replications and internalizations observable in adult behavior. Presenting a case analysis, Benjamin used the MCMI to document changes in personality and the INTREX questionnaires to document associated changes in perception of object relations after long-term psychotherapy.

These are the only published reports illustrating the combined use of objective tests into an objective test battery.

The remainder of this chapter illustrates, clinically, the process and value of combining the MCMI-II with other objective personality tests.

Case #1

The patient is a 41-year-old, separated, unemployed black male who was voluntarily admitted to an inpatient psychiatric treatment unit following a suicide attempt. He was placed on short-term antidepressant therapy and then transferred to an inpatient drug treatment rehabilitation program within the same facility.

The patient used alcohol and marijuana episodically since high school, apparently without problems. He began to freebase cocaine about a year and a half ago, resulting in rapid social and vocational deterioration. At the time of admission he was homeless, no longer able to maintain full-time employment, had a history of being taken advantage of by others, and had made two suicide attempts. The first suicide attempt was occasioned when his live-in girlfriend left him for another man. He experienced a Major Depression and attempted suicide by taking an overdose of drugs. It was unsuccessful and he remained in his apartment for two weeks, eventually returning to emotional equilibrium without psychiatric treatment. His most recent attempt was by drowning, except he said he got too cold in the water and swam back to shore. He tried to get himself arrested on petty charges so he would have a place to stay and be fed, but the police transported him for emergency psychiatric treatment.

His MCMI-II profile code is 8B8A26A with elevations also on 6B and 5. His Scale X score suggests endorsement of a wide number of problems, perhaps to bring attention to his problems. The high-ranging code, with a large number of scale elevations, reflects serious psychological maladjustment. He is seen as negativistic, bitter, resentful, angry, moody, faultfinding, stubborn, and passive-aggressive (8A). In addition, he permits himself to be exploited, taken advantage of, or abused. He may act in ways designed to undo the good that people try to do for him, and acts like a person who has suffered and been victimized throughout life. His many complaints and martyr-like conversations tend to demoralize those around him, who lose patience with his obstructionistic behavior (8B). Behind this negativistic and self-defeating behavior is a deeply dependent individual who is conflicted between self-assertion and his needs for dependency (2). His substance abuse may serve to reduce his tensions, contain his impulses, and reduce his frustrations. However, it also reinforces his underlying dependence and perpetuates his self-defeating cycle of behavior. Substance abuse and depression are clinical symptoms suggested by the profile.

Table 5.1A
41-year-old Black Male

	MCMI-II Scale Scores		
Scales	BR Scores	Scales	BR Scores
X	97	S	67
Y	62	C	98
Z	75	P	93
1	76	A	57
2	104	H	44
3	64	N	65
4	66	D	77
5	91	B	90
6a	102	t	96
6b	96	ss	75
7	52	cc	61
8a	106	pp	64
8b	109		

Table 5.1B
41-year-old Black Male

	MMPI-2 Scale Scores				
Scales	T Scores	Scales	T Scores	Scales	T Scores
L	52	ANX	67	WRK	65
F	76	FRS	64	TRT	69
K	41	OBS	66	MAC-R	R36
Hs	51	DEP	83	A	70
Dep	72	HEA	58	R	58
Hy	50	BIX	67	Es	30
Pd	90	ANG	67		
Mf	56	Cyn	71		
Pa	64	ASP	72		
Pt	66	TPA	68		
Sc	77	LSE	59		
Ma	65	SOD	60		
Si	59	FAM	74		

His MMPI-2 code (482796') is also high ranging and also suggests serious emotional trouble. The profile suggests he is moody, resentful, angry (F, 4, 8), feels inadequate and insecure (2), alienated and misunderstood (8), is depressed (2, DEP), and reports a number of family problems (FAM) and anti-social practices (4, ASP). Additionally, he seems to be experiencing residual symptoms of a psychotic-like nature (8, BIZ) which may be drug induced (4, MAC-R). He seems to be a dependent individual (2, Do) when not acting out or using drugs. Depression and substance abuse are the most prominent clinical symptoms suggested by the profile.

Integration. Consensual validity is found in that both tests assess him as moody and erratic with underlying dependence associated with his acting-out and impulsive behavior. The MCMI-II tapped the self-defeating aspect while the MMPI-2 tapped his residual psychotic symptoms. Substance abuse and depression are reflected in both tests.

Case #2

Patient is a 34-year-old, employed, white male in marital therapy. When he was age 10, his mother left home with another man, who was alcoholic, leaving her ex-husband to raise the children. His father worked two jobs to financially survive, resulting in less supervision of his children, who began to engage in various delinquent activities. The patient later married and also began to work two jobs to save for a house. His wife began to feel neglected and had a brief affair, which he learned about. This affair reawakened his repressed memories and angry feelings over maternal rejection. Perhaps in unconscious retaliation, he had an affair, which was the direct precipitant for the couple seeking marital counseling. His therapist reports that the patient has many antisocial characteristics and associated residual traits, which are mostly contained in daily behavior but which emerge when he feels threatened or provoked. His test results appear in Table 5.2A & B.

Table 5.2A
34-year-old, Married, White Male

MCMI-II Scale Scores			
Scales	BR Scores	Scales	BR Scores
X	72	S	67
Y	30	C	64
Z	78	P	71
1	88	A	85
2	85	H	61
3	00	N	35
4	36	D	88
5	61	B	63
6A	94	T	70
6B	102	SS	75
7	61	CC	68
8A	107	PP	67
8B	65		

ROBERT J. CRAIG, PH.D.

Table 5.2B
34-year-old, Married, White Male

MMPI-2 Scale Scores					
Scales	*T* Scores	Scales	*T* Scores	Scales	*T* Scores
L	43	ANX	60	WRK	46
F	48	FRS	35	TRT	56
K	49	OBS	53	MAC-R	R23
Hs	45	DEP	51	A	49
Dep	40	HEA	51	R	36
Hy	43	BIZ	60	Es	47
Pd	62	ANG	70	MDS	68
Mf	62	Cyn	59		
Pa	53	ASP	72		
Pt	59	TPA	72		
Sc	56	LSE	41		
Ma	75	SOD	55		
Si	55	FAM	80		

His MCMI-II profile is a 8A6B6A12 high-ranging code, suggesting maladjustment. The negativistic and erratic components to his personality appear pre-potent. He would be described as negativistic, pessimistic, temperamental, and unpredictable, with much underlying anger and resentment. Such patients have a potential for assaultive behavior. However, he tries to control his anger and hostility through the use of passive-aggressive and/or obstructionistic behaviors. He is strongly opinionated and stubborn. Millon's theory of this negativistic style asserts that such patients anticipate being disillusioned by others and so they behave in an uncooperative manner to avoid disappointments. Thus, he probably has a chip-on-the-shoulder demeanor and an argumentative and complaining emotional stance. His interpersonal relationships are likely to be quite problematic. A general belligerence and uncooperativeness can be expected of him. Anxiety and depression are the prominent clinical states.

His MMPI-2 profile is a one-point code (9'), indicating he is hyperactive, agitated, narcissistic, easily bored and frustrated, impulsive, and moody. He is likely to be manipulative, and he reports problems in the areas of anger (ANG), antisocial practices (ASP), and family difficulties (FAM). The Marital Distress Scale (MDS) is also elevated.

Integration. Both tests reflect his anger, low tolerance for frustration, agitation, impulsivity, and moodiness. Both suggest antisocial traits and interpersonal difficulties. In this author's opinion the MCMI-II provides a more refined clinical description of his personality style.

Case #3

This patient is a 64-year-old, divorced, white male in outpatient psychotherapy. He was referred for aftercare services by his psychiatrists following a 3-week admission on a psychiatric ward. Upon hospital admission he was agitated, depressed, anxious, and hallucinatory, with homicidal impulses toward his children, all of whom are married.

He is a retired dentist, who sold his practice in order to have more regular working hours. He had arranged a part-time job with another dental practice as an employee. This did not work out, because he was expected to "sell" dental services in addition to servicing clients. He found this unpalatable and he was terminated. Since then he has been unable to find a job.

He has a small income from the sale of his practice, but is having financial problems and has no insurance.

He was married for over 30 years, but his wife died from cancer. He had five children, but one died in a plane crash about 15 years ago. He remarried about 3 years after his wife's death, but this didn't work out, because his children were against the relationship; he later divorced.

He has been anxious throughout much of his life and has been dependent on tranquilizers and anxiolytics for about 25 years. Previous efforts to detox from these drugs have been unsuccessful. He also has a history of two previous psychiatric admissions for Major Depression and was treated with electric shock therapy.

The patient paints as a hobby. Prior to the most recent psychiatric episode, he drew a picture of a tiger and noticed the animal had an enraged expression on its face, as if ready to attack. Also, while on the phone talking to his daughter, he drove a knife through her picture. These two events scared him and were followed by a hallucination and homicidal ideation; he then voluntarily sought treatment. Most recently he has shown a proclivity toward compulsive handwashing, up to 4 hours a day, which he justifies through erudite treatises on bacteria. His test results are depicted in Table 5.3A & B.

The MCMI-II code is 78A, reflecting compulsive and passive-aggressive personality traits. Configural interpretation of this code suggests that his behavior is replete with conflicted hostility, a pretense of composure, anxious defensiveness against criticism, but strong judgmental attitudes toward others. Although he wishes to redress past perceived grievances with supporting arguments and data that he believes prove his contentions, he generally suppresses his resentments, striving, instead, to act in a proper, conforming, and well-disciplined manner. Displays of warmth, gentleness, and intimacy are avoided.

Rather, he tends to lecture on proper conduct. He is prone, however, to erupt in sudden outbursts of temper that he usually rationalizes. The test shows a strong compulsive aspect to his behavior (7). Depression is the major clinically significant symptom.

Table 5.3A
64-year-old, Divorced, White Male

MCMI-II Scale Scores

Scales	BR Scores	Scales	BR Scores
X	60	S	57
Y	56	C	70
Z	52	P	64
1	60	A	45
2	67	H	72
3	66	N	39
4	47	D	88
5	66	B	62
6A	47	T	51
6B	62	SS	60
7	90	CC	60
8A	81	PP	55
8B	72		

Table 5.3B
64-year-old, Divorced, White Male

MMPI-2 Scale Scores

Scales	T Scores	Scales	T Scores	Scales	T Scores
L	43	ANX	67	WRK	67
F	55	FRS	67	TRT	61
K	49	OBS	63	MAC-R	R21
Hs	77	DEP	66	A	67
Dep	72	HEA	76	R	50
Hy	74	BIZ	70	Es	31
Pd	54	ANG	56	APS	54
Mf	60	Cyn	51	AAS	42
Pa	72	ASP	49	Do	51
Pt	74	TPA	56	O-H	45
Sc	94	LSE	59	Sc6	104
Ma	65	SOD	55		
Si	57	FAM	71		

The patient's MMPI-2 code is a high-ranging profile reflecting his continuing problems with intense anxiety (7, ANX), anger (8), agitation and depression (8, 2, DEP), and somatic distress (1, 2, HEA). He appears to be suspicious (6), if not delusional (BIZ), and he endorsed a number of items pertaining to the presence of delusions and hallucinations, poor memory, and problems in concentration (BIZ, Sc6). He is plagued by anxiety and preoccupied with feeling guilty and unworthy. He has difficulty managing routine affairs and shows little energy (2, DEP). Given his history, it is interesting that his Anger content scale was average.

Integration. The MMPI-2 seemed to present a more accurate assessment of this patient's symptom picture than that suggested by the MCMI-II. It tapped into his psychotic symptoms, problems with agitation, anxiety, fears, somatic concerns, and energy level. The MCMI-II seemed to present a more accurate description of his basic personality style. Both tests adequately assessed his depression and problems with compulsive behavior. Anger management seems to be a central issue in therapy (recall that the object of his anger was his children), but he reported few symptoms of anger on the MMPI-2 Anger content scale, suggesting his continuing wish to deny and suppress these emotions. The MCMI-II suggests that he channels these impulses into passive-aggressive and compulsive behaviors.

Case #4

This is a 40-year-old, divorced, white male in outpatient psychotherapy. He initially sought clinical services for marital problems associated with his continuous alcoholic drinking. His wife eventually divorced him and later bore a child; the patient had been unable to father a child because of low sperm count, perhaps due to heavy marijuana use. His previous therapist had tried, unsuccessfully, to get him into an alcoholic rehabilitation treatment program, but he refused this treatment approach. The therapist left the practice and the case was reassigned.

At time of transfer the patient was evaluated as depressed, anxious, self-defeating, and a gamma alcoholic. Again, the primary goal was to motivate the patient to enter alcohol rehabilitation.

Although the patient never appeared to be intoxicated, he always came to the therapy sessions with an odor of alcohol on his breath (as he had done with his previous therapist). He drank primarily vodka and beer during his lunch hour, after work in sports bars, and at his girlfriend's house. He was under treatment for alcoholic fatty liver, but had no other medical problems. He had a secure job and seemed to maintain a variety of enabling relationships in his immediate social surround that helped to maintain his drinking.

While in therapy, he was innocently engaged by a group of Hispanic teenagers, one of whom spat on him, while he was waiting at a stoplight. He impulsively grabbed one by the head and stepped on the gas, intending to "drag him to death." The youth slipped out of the hold and ran away. The event occasioned a high-speed car chase with the patient pursuing the group of youths in a car. They pulled into an alley and jumped out in a threatening manner. The patient backed off and went home.

Throughout his therapy sessions, which he attended irregularly, he presented a myriad of rationalizations as to why he could not enter alcohol rehab. As these reasons were challenged, he dreamed up yet one excuse after another. His alcoholism had caused the dissolution of his marriage, was beginning to affect his liver, and was partially responsible for his impulsive and thoughtless behavior that could have resulted in charges of aggravated battery and even attempted murder, had the last incident led to an arrest. The patient was unwilling to enter alcohol treatment but was willing to undergo a more thorough psychological evaluation. He was given the *Michigan Alcoholism Screening Test* to provide some objective evidence of his alcoholism, the *Wechsler Memory Scale* to assess the effects of drinking on memory processes, and the MCMI-II, the MMPI-2, and the 16PF to evaluate the extent of psychological symptoms and personality traits. His scores appear in Table 5.4A, B, & C.

His MCMI-II code type is 6B8A6A reflecting aggressive, passive-aggressive, and antisocial traits. The passive-aggressive component to his personality suggests an unpredictable mood, a bitter and resentful irritability, and a mistrusting and gloomy outlook on life. Such personalities can become impulsive and openly hostile and tend to spend much of the time being negative, faultfinding, stubborn, grumbling, and complaining. The antisocial component, in combination with the passive-aggressive component, suggests he is resentful, often dissatisfied, touchy, broods over perceived slights, and probably presents with angry and hostile affect. Because his history reveals little antisocial or aggressive behaviors, it is speculated that his drinking may serve, in part, a function of containing his deep resentments and hostility, which may erupt during periods of sobriety. The elevation on the Borderline scale is probably due to his changeable and erratic emotionality, chronic anger and resentment, and depressive affect which is also part of a Borderline personality organization. Also, he is sensitive to perceived rejection (2). Symptomatically, he reports substance abuse, depression, and some anxiety. Millon's theory asserts that his basic conflict is between dependence and self-assertion.

Table 5.4A
40-year-old, Divorced, White Male

MCMI-II Scale Scores

Scales	BR Scores	Scales	BR Scores
X	77	S	64
Y	25	C	93
Z	80	P	65
1	74	A	78
2	78	H	55
3	21	N	58
4	61	D	88
5	71	B	93
6A	83	T	87
6B	112	SS	60
7	34	CC	66
8A	111	PP	50
8B	73		

Table 5.4B
40-year-old, Divorced, White Male

MMPI-2 Scale Scores

Scales	T Scores	Scales	T Scores	Scales	T Scores
L	39	ANX	65	WRK	67
F	55	FRS	45	TRT	56
K	45	OBS	59	MAC-R	R29
Hs	59	DEP	77	A	65
Dep	74	HEA	48	R	47
Hy	66	BIX	63	Es	40
Pd	67	ANG	78	APS	73
Mf	46	Cyn	48	AAS	80
Pa	72	ASP	51	Do	58
Pt	66	TPA	56	O-H	35
Sc	62	LSE	53	D1	82
Ma	56	SOD	50	Hy3	93
Si	51	FAM	74	Pd5	82

The MMPI-2 shows him to be passive-aggressive (scales 4, 5, 6), depressed (2), and angry and sullen (4) with little direction or purpose in life (4, 6). He feels alienated, pessimistic, insecure, and inadequate (2). He appears to harbor much resentment (4, 5, 6), tends to be critical of others, and is quite suspicious (6). Symptomatically, he reports difficulties with

ROBERT J. CRAIG, PH.D.

depression (2, D1, Hy3, Pd5), anger (4, ANG), and family problems (4, FAM). Additionally, substance abuse is also indicated by the test results (MAC-R, AAS, APS).

Table 5.4C
40-year-old, Divorced, White Male

	16 PF Scores			
	Factors	STEN Score	Needs	STEN Score
A	Warmth	2	ABA	4
B	Abstract Thinking	5	ACH	8
C	Calm, Stable	6	AFF	2
E	Dominant	9	AGG	9
F	Enthusiastic	6	AUT	8
G	Conscientious	5	CHA	5
H	Venturesome	6	DEF	3
I	Sensitive	5	DOM	7
L	Suspicious	8	END	5
M	Imaginative	6	EXH	7
N	Shrewd	3	HET	7
O	Self-Doubting	6	INT	3
Q1	Experimenting	1	NUR	3
Q2	Self-Sufficient	6	ORD	4
Q3	Self-Disciplined	4	SUC	8
Q4	Tense, Driven	10		

The 16PF shows him to be jealous, suspicious, mistrusting, irritable, oppositional, resentful, and hostile (L), tense, frustrated, driven, and anxious (Q4), socially withdrawn and seclusive, lacking in warmth, cool and aloof, and passive in interpersonal relations. He is likely to have conflicted family interactions (A). He tends to use displacement and projection as primary defenses (L) and is seen as controlling (E). Elevated scores on factor E are often associated with conflicts with a need to be dominant and assertive and a need for dependence—a conflict also suggested by the MCMI-II. He harbors guilt (O) and may be impulsive (F). Interestingly, the low score on Q1 is often seen in people who find it difficult to change. (When asked early in treatment how likely it was that he would discontinue alcohol abuse on a 1-10 scale with 1 reflecting "no chance," he immediately responded with a rating of 5 [reflecting his ambivalence], then thought a moment and said, "No, 3.")

His need pattern, computer-derived from the 16PF, shows that he has high needs for aggression, achievement, autonomy, exhibition, and succorance (dependence), and low needs for affiliation, deference, intraception (self-understanding), and nurturance. How can a person have both high needs for dominance and autonomy and a high need for dependence? Once again we see a conflict between a need for dependence and a need for self-assertion. His low needs for affiliation and nurturance, combined with his high needs for dominance and autonomy, would suggest that interpersonal relationships are used primarily to gratify his own needs.

Integration. Both the MCMI-II and the MMPI-2 reflect his depression, irritability, passive-aggressive personality style, problems with suspiciousness and mistrust, resentments, and anger. All three tests reflect more problems with aggression than are evident from his history. Perhaps his passive-aggressive personality style, combined with the depressant effects of alcohol, serves to control these impulses. All tests reflect his resentment, anxiety, lack of trust, and suspiciousness. They also corroborate the lack of warmth this man displays in his daily behavior.

Case #5

The patient is a 28-year-old, married, white male who sought counseling services for marital problems. He has been married for 3 years, has one child, and is employed full-time in the construction industry. He has a high school education.

His wife had recently left him and indicated that she wanted a divorce. Since then he experienced a 16-pound weight loss, problematic sleep (delayed sleep onset and frequent night awakenings), episodic crying, anxiety, and mild suicidal ideation.

He reported that his wife complained about his temper, possessiveness, and jealousy (adding that he has nightmares of learning that his wife is having an affair), verbal abuse, mental cruelty, and his reluctance to socialize. They argued frequently, mostly about financial matters. She left him about five times in their 3-year marriage, each time staying away for longer periods of time. She had seen a lawyer but had not filed divorce papers.

Upon the initial interview, he presented with some impulsivity, sensitivity to rejection, and dependent and clinging behavior, but with an overall sincerity. Possessiveness, jealousy, and temper were judged to be the main behavioral problems. He admits he had these same problems with other women in his life. The patient's test results are presented in Table 5.5A & B.

Table 5.5A
28-year-old, Separated, White Male

MCMI-II Scale Scores			
Scales	BR Scores	Scales	BR Scores
X	60	S	67
Y	56	C	61
Z	78	P	43
1	76	A	74
2	87	H	56
3	69	N	84
4	36	D	84
5	19	B	45
6A	27	T	48
6B	41	SS	61
7	64	CC	66
8A	81	PP	44
8B	74		

Table 5.5B
28-year-old, Separated, White Male

16 PF Scores		
	Factors	STEN Score
A	Warmth	4
B	Abstract Thinking	8
C	Calm, Stable	4
E	Dominant	9
F	Enthusiastic	4
G	Conscientious	4
H	Venturesome	1
I	Sensitive	9
L	Suspicious	10
M	Imaginative	4
N	Shrewd	6
O	Self-Doubting	10
Q1	Experimenting	1
Q2	Self-Sufficient	8
Q3	Self-Disciplined	1
Q4	Tense, Driven	10

The patient's MCMI-II code is 28A1. The 28A code, as described in Chapter 2, depicts him as sensitive to rejection, uncomfortable in social situations, nervous in interpersonal situations, and tending to be a loner. Any serious relationship is likely to be conflictual due to the patient's vacillation between friendly and cooperative behaviors and negativistic, hostile, and obstructionistic behaviors. He is sensitive to criticism and censure and prone to sudden outbursts of anger. Depression is the major clinical symptom.

His 16PF profile depicts him as a person who is jealous and suspicious, has an anxious insecurity, and displaces and projects his emotions (L). He is highly tense and anxious, driven, and volatile (probably due to situational anxiety precipitated by the marital separation) (Q4), and feels inadequate and unworthy. He worries needlessly, is easily overcome by his moods, is sensitive to approval/disapproval, and tends to spend much time brooding (O). He has a strong need to be controlling, is stubborn, demanding, excitable, and prone to jealousy (E). He is easily upset (C), shy and withdrawn, sensitive to threat with feelings of inferiority (H), immature (Q3), and quite cautious, serious, and dour in demeanor (F).

Integration. Both tests establish his sensitivity to rejection and his problematic and conflicted relationships (inferred from 16PF score pattern). Each test, the MCMI-II and the 16PF, adds dimensions to his personality that are not tapped by the other, thereby enriching the description of his personality.

Case #6

Patient is a 30-year-old, employed, white male in outpatient psychotherapy. He has remarried and is involved in a bitter dispute with his ex-wife over physical custody of his son. His ex-wife currently has custody, but the patient has filed for custody, claiming his ex-wife is an unfit mother. She has, in turn, taken him to court on multiple occasions on a variety of charges. She claimed the child was sexually abused and obtained a restraining order prohibiting visitation. The charges were subsequently dropped for lack of evidence. She has taken the child to several different physicians for a variety of alleged physical problems, but the patient insists there is nothing wrong with the child—a finding apparently substantiated by the physicians. She has accused him of trying to run her over with his car in a parking lot and produced a witness who was the mother of her new boyfriend, but the patient denies this and claims it was a setup. At trial, he was judged not guilty. He has been prohibited from taking the child out of state and, when he took him on a small vacation to a neighboring

ROBERT J. CRAIG, PH.D.

state for a few days, his ex-wife learned of the trip and took him to court on a contempt citation. She charged him with physical assault during their marriage; he was arrested, but charges were dropped. He sought psychotherapy to help him deal with his anger at his ex-wife and at the judicial system for going along with her false charges. After he gets custody, he plans to sue his ex-wife for malicious prosecution and to sue a psychologist—who saw his son as part of the sexual abuse charges and hinted that perhaps the charges were true—for malpractice. The custody court hearing was approaching and the therapist wanted more objective evidence in case he was called to testify in the case. There was a 16PF and an MCMI-II already in file; the patient was then given the MMPI-2. His test results appear in Table 5.6A, B, & C.

Table 5.6A
30-year-old, Married, White Male

MCMI-II Scale Scores			
Scales	BR Scores	Scales	BR Scores
X	63	S	43
Y	67	C	66
Z	35	P	60
1	13	A	18
2	44	H	46
3	50	N	60
4	83	D	18
5	98	B	55
6A	83	T	65
6B	89	SS	44
7	61	CC	35
8A	66	PP	38
8B	47		

His MCMI-II profile is a 56B code with secondary elevations on 4 and 6A. This profile suggests a strong egocentricity, an inflated sense of self, arrogance, and independent and competitive traits. He is likely to be both aggressive and assertive, going after what he wants for himself at the expense of others' needs. There is little antisocial activity in his history except for a brief period of cocaine abuse, which has been in remission now for several years. The MCMI-II suggests no clinical syndrome, and his personality issues warrant the most therapeutic attention. Because anger is the major presenting complaint, elevations on scales 6A and 6B are probably due to endorsing many items associated with this characteristic.

Table 5.6B
30-year-old, Married, White Male

16 PF Scores

	Factors	STEN Score
A	Warmth	2
B	Abstract Thinking	10
C	Calm, Stable	6
E	Dominant	8
F	Enthusiastic	8
G	Conscientious	8
H	Venturesome	10
I	Sensitive	1
L	Suspicious	4
M	Imaginative	2
N	Shrewd	4
O	Self-Doubting	8
Q1	Experimenting	2
Q2	Self-Sufficient	8
Q3	Self-Disciplined	6
Q4	Tense, Driven	8

Table 5.6C
30-year-old, Married, White Male

MMPI-2 Scale Scores

Scales	T Scores	Scales	T Scores	Scales	T Scores
L	56	ANX	47	WRK	36
F	42	FRS	35	TRT	39
K	58	OBS	33	MAC-R	RXX
Hs	45	DEP	45	A	36
Dep	36	HEA	37	R	45
Hy	52	BIZ	51	Es	60
Pd	44	ANG	48	MAC-R	R20
Mf	52	Cyn	47	O-H	69
Pa	64	ASP	42		
Pt	39	TPA	41		
Sc	39	LSE	41		
Ma	56	SOD	39		
Si	36	FAM	41		

His MMPI-2 test results, given after about a year of therapy, is a Within Normal Limits code. Again, no clinical syndrome is evidenced from the profile, and he seems to be experiencing an overall positive adjustment. Although his Anger scale is Normal, his overcontrolled hostility (O-H) is elevated. He shows signs of being oversensitive and suspicious (6). These traits, combined with the suppression of hostility, may make him vulnerable to developing stress-related disorders. This style can be explained on the basis of his wife's behavior and his reactions to it.

His 16PF shows him to be highly intelligent (B), dominant (E), bold (H), tough-minded (I), independent (Q2), having some self-doubts (O) and tension (Q4), but also forthrightness (N).

Integration. The MCMI-II and 16PF both show him to have an independent personality style that seems well suited for his vocation as a stockbroker and trader. Both the MCMI-II and the MMPI-2 suggest a general absence of clinical syndromes except for suppressed hostility, indicated on the MMPI-2. Of special importance are the normal limits profile on the MMPI-2, the validity scales in the normal range on the MMPI-2 and on the MCMI-II, and a high score on Forthright (N) on the 16PF, all suggesting that he is telling the truth with respect to his ex-wife's behavior and his response to it. This case also illustrates the general principal that personality evaluation is improved when the clinician combines test results with known aspects of the case and the person.

Case #7

This patient is a 24-year-old, single, white male employed in the computer industry. He initially sought services due to work-related problems. He reported that his family and social life were in order, but he was having anxiety attacks and feelings of inadequacy and inferiority associated with work-related activities. He has a college degree in business and, after a 6-month training period, he was sent out on jobs as the company's main representative, installing computer programs and training staff in their use. This often entailed interaction with high-level corporate executives and private entrepreneurs. He had great difficulty relating to them, believing he was inferior to them and feeling he couldn't relate to them. He sought counseling services to help him with interpersonal skills in the work environment. His test results appear in Table 5.7A & B.

Table 5.7A
24-year-old, Single, White Male

MCMI-II Scale Scores

Scales	BR Scores	Scales	BR Scores
X	60	S	70
Y	67	C	64
Z	82	P	65
1	69	A	126
2	74	H	79
3	89	N	47
4	06	D	108
5	35	B	67
6A	27	T	41
6B	49	SS	62
7	90	CC	71
8A	67	PP	53
8B	65		

Table 5.7B
24-year-old, Single, White Male

CPI Scores

Scales	Standard Score	Scales	Standard Score
Dominant	63	Achievement via Conformance	49
Capacity for Status	47	Achievement via Independence	55
Sociability	51	Intellectual Efficiency	56
Social Poise	62	Psychological-Mindedness	51
Self-Acceptance	60	Flexibility	42
Independence	39	Femininity/Masculinity	45
Empathy	48	Alpha, V 2	NA
Responsibility	57		
Socialization	58		
Self-Control	42		
Good Impression	47		
Communality	58		
Well-Being	51		
Tolerance	61		

His MCMI-II code is 73, emphasizing compulsive and dependent traits. He is both conforming and dependent. His salient traits include high needs for achievement, behavioral rigidity, conforming behaviors, conscientiousness, and perfectionism. He relates in a submissive style, which is meant to protect him against criticism and from his own repressed hostility and resentment. His self-image is one of correctness and propriety. By conforming he can secure the approval from others that he seeks. He tends to avoid criticism by presenting a superficially friendly and compliant behavior, but is likely to be guarded and defensive about his personal problems.

The results of the California Psychological Inventory (CPI) show him to be in the Alpha V.2 quadrant, reflecting a person who tends to be ambitious, outgoing, enterprising, assertive, norm favoring, rule abiding, and supportive of social mores. However, with a V.2 score, he is not very actualized in these traits. Although he has inherently good leadership skills, they are not fully utilized.

The Class I scales (Do through Em), reflect good interpersonal skills. He has a sense of confidence and assertion (Do), social poise (Sp), and is at ease in most social situations (Sa). He presents himself well and can either take the initiative or defer to others, depending on the circumstances. He can get along reasonably well with others (Sy) and is likely to be quite cheerful. However, he doubts his own abilities, tends to avoid situations where he has to make decisions, and seeks the help and support of others, probably to avoid responsibility for mistakes and to avoid the disapproval of authority (as suggested by the MCMI-II profile).

The Class II scales (Re through To) suggest that he tries to be fair-minded, tolerant (To), conscientious, dutiful, and takes his obligations seriously (Re). He is industrious and reliable but overconforming and lacking imagination (So). At heart, he likes excitement and adventure and wants the freedom to express ideas without fear of disapproval (Sc). He takes a rational and realistic view of everyday problems (Wb).

The Class III scales (Ac through Ie) suggest he applies himself well and enjoys the challenge of new problems (Ie), and that he is clear-thinking and analytical, particularly in independent situations (Ai).

The Class IV scales (Py through FM) show that he is too cautious and inhibited and needs to loosen up and enjoy life (particularly in the work setting) (Fx), especially as he seems to enjoy competition and challenge and has the capacity to be assertive (F/M).

Integration. The CPI confirms what was suggested by the MCMI-II, but puts it in terms of working relationships. His inhibitions, self-doubts, and excessive worries as to the approval of authority figures seem to get in the way of personal fulfillment. This personality style has interfered with his desire for career advancement. Interestingly, this patient was very comfortable, assertive, and confident outside of working relationships, perhaps because of the absence of authority figures who could not judge his behavior.

Case #8

This patient is a 36-year-old, married, white female in outpatient psycho-therapy. She is married with four children and sought marital counseling. She complained of her husband's drinking, considers him a poor financial provider and wants him to work two jobs, and feels he doesn't understand her. She is employed part-time, and her father was alcoholic. She alleges her husband beats her, yells, screams, and punches her, and is overly forceful in disciplining the children. She says she has hit and scratched him as well. She admits she nags him too much, but says she can't help it and besides, she adds, it's for her husband's "own good." She called her therapist one evening to report her husband had physically abused her. The following day, they both came for a counseling session. He was badly beaten and scratched, with many facial abrasions, while she had no evidence of physical assault. Husband said he was only trying to defend himself and that he merely tried to block her punches and restrain her arms. Her therapist evaluated her in a clinical inter-view as mildly histrionic and possibly depressed. Her test results appear in Table 5.8A & B.

Her MCMI-II code is 6B4, of moderate severity and intensity (*BR*=78). The code suggests that, although she is superficially friendly and sociable, she has problems controlling her temper, and family members would probably attest to the fact that she is generally irritable, argumentative, moody, overly dramatic, and impulsive. She is capable of intimidating others through verbal abuse and probably has a sharp tongue. When things don't go her way, she uses her anger to control others with temper outbursts, vindictive anger, and uncontrollable rage. In short, the MCMI-II suggests that she is a spouse abuser.

The 16PF describes her as tense and driven (Q4), anxious, and a person who is easily overcome by moods. She feels inadequate (O), has strong needs to control others, to be authoritative, and demanding (E), with low superego con-trols (G), seems to experience little fun in life and is unnecessarily serious (F), yet is dominated by external realities, concerned with the immediate situation, and anxious to do the right thing (in her terms) (M).

ROBERT J. CRAIG, PH.D.

Table 5.8A
36-year-old, Married, White Female

MCMI-II Scale Scores

Scales	BR Scores	Scales	BR Scores
X	60	S	46
Y	75	C	73
Z	54	P	67
1	66	A	37
2	69	H	59
3	75	N	67
4	78	D	63
5	47	B	70
6A	66	T	62
6B	78	SS	60
7	61	CC	60
8A	74	PP	60
8B	75		

Table 5.8B
36-year-old, Married, White Female

16 PF Scores

	Factors	STEN Score
A	Warmth	6
B	Abstract Thinking	4
C	Calm, Stable	6
E	Dominant	8
F	Enthusiastic	1
G	Conscientious	4
H	Venturesome	8
I	Sensitive	1
L	Suspicious	4
M	Imaginative	1
N	Shrewd	8
O	Self-Doubting	10
Q1	Experimenting	2
Q2	Self-Sufficient	2
Q3	Self-Disciplined	6
Q4	Tense, Driven	10

Integration. Both tests describe a psychological portrait of an individual who would be prone to dominating and physically abusing her partner. She is married to a man whose test results indicated that he is a dependent personality, and this union allows her to intimidate, dominate, and control him through both verbal and physical means.

Case #9

This is a 51-year-old, married, white female in marital therapy. Her husband complains that she nags too much, doesn't enjoy life, is overly critical, sexually cold, and has few interests and few friends. He reports she is unduly jealous when he talks with other women, is too crabby, keeps the house in a cluttered condition, and is a bitter and demanding person. Her test results appear in Table 5.9A & B.

Table 5.9A
51-year-old, Married, White Female

MCMI-II Scale Scores			
Scales	BR Scores	Scales	BR Scores
X	55	S	45
Y	41	C	51
Z	45	P	39
1	67	A	00
2	73	H	30
3	66	N	55
4	61	D	10
5	38	B	39
6A	58	T	48
6B	76	SS	35
7	64	CC	50
8A	69	PP	00
8B	42		

Her MCMI-II code is 6B, with a secondary elevation on 2. This profile suggests a person who is stern and judgmental, self-righteous, and conflicted about her underlying hostility, of which she may be unaware. It is likely that she learned to be this way and carries an unconscious desire to vindicate past humiliations and perceived grievances. She avoids displays of warmth and intimacy and maintains a harsh exterior. Her resentments break through in sudden outbursts of anger that she later rationalizes.

Table 5.9B
51-year-old, Married, White Female

	16 PF Scores	
	Factors	STEN Score
A	Warmth	1
B	Abstract Thinking	9
C	Ego Strength	9
E	Dominant	4
F	Impulsivity	6
G	Group Conformity	8
H	Boldness	1
I	Tender-Minded	2
L	Suspiciousness	6
M	Imagination	2
N	Shrewdness	10
O	Guilt Proneness	10
Q1	Rebelliousness	4
Q2	Self-Sufficiency	8
Q3	Compulsivity	4
Q4	Free-Floating	8

The 16PF validates her husband's description of her personality. This woman appears as very retiring, introverted, withdrawn, distrustful, rigid, lacking in warmth, sensitive to threat, and lacking confidence (A, H). She is emotionally detached (N) yet easily overcome by moods and is prone to become dejected, particularly when criticized (O). An intelligent woman (B), she is conservative and would find change difficult (Q1). She tends to hide her feelings when emotionally upset (C).

Integration. Both tests suggest a lack of warmth, intimacy, and emotional attachment in close relationships. The MCMI-II adds the concept that she tries to dominate and control intimate relationships through harsh, stern, and judgmental behaviors. It also suggests a dynamic reason for those behaviors.

Antoni, M. H. (1993). The combined use of the MCMI and MMPI. In. R. J. Craig (Ed.). *The Millon Clinical Multiaxial Inventory: A clinical research information synthesis* (pp. 279-302). Hillsdale, NJ: Lawrence Erlbaum.

Antoni, M. H., Levine, J., Tischer, P., Green, C., & Millon, T. (1985a). Refining MMPI code interpretations by reference to MCMI scale data, part I: MMPI Code 28/82. *Journal of Personality Assessment, 49,* 392-398.

Antoni, M. H., Levine, J., Tischer, P., Green, C., & Millon, T. (1985b). Refining assessments by combining MCMI high point profiles and MMPI codes, part III: MMPI Code 24/42. *Journal of Personality Assessment, 49,* 508-515.

Antoni, M. H., Levine, J., Tischer, P., Green, C., & Millon, T. (1986). Refining personality assessments by combining MCMI high point profiles and MMPI codes, part IV: MMPI Code 89/98. *Journal of Personality Assessment, 50,* 65-72.

Antoni, M. H., Levine, J., Tischer, P., Green, C., & Millon, T. (1987). Refining personality assessment by combining MCMI high point profiles and MMPI codes, Part V: MMPI Code 78/87. *Journal of Personality Assessment, 51,* 375-387.

Benjamin, L. S. (1974). Structural Analysis of Social Behavior. *Psychological Review, 81,* 392-425.

Benjamin, L. S. (1984). Principles of prediction using Structural Analysis of Social Behavior. In R. A. Zucker, J. Aronoff, and A. J. Rabin (Eds.). *Personality and the prediction of behavior.* New York: Academic Press.

Benjamin, L. S. (1987). Combined use of the MCMI and the SASB intrex questionnaires to document and facilitate personality change during long-term psychotherapy. In C. Green (Ed.). *Conference on the Millon Clinical Inventories (MCMI, MBHI, MAPI)* (pp. 305-323). Minneapolis: National Computer Systems.

Craig, R. J. (Ed.). (1993). *The Millon Clinical Multiaxial Inventory: A clinical research information synthesis.* Hillsdale, NJ: Lawrence Erlbaum.

Hyer, L., Woods, M. G., Boudewyns, P. A., Harrison, W. R., & Tamkin, A. S. (1990). MCMI and 16PF with Vietnam veterans: Profiles and concurrent validation of MCMI. *Journal of Personality Disorders, 4,* 391-401.

Levine, J., Antoni, M. H., Tischer, P., Green, C., & Millon, T. (1985). Refining MMPI code interpretations by reference to MCMI scale data, part II: MMPI Code 27/72. *Journal of Personality Assessment, 49,* 501-507.

Levine, J., Tischer, P., Antoni, M. H., Green, C., & Millon, T. (1985). Refining personality assessments by combining MCMI high point profiles and MMPI codes, part VI: MMPI Code 49/94. *Journal of Personality Assessment, 49,* 501-507.

Morey, L. C., Waugh, M. H., & Blashfield, R. K. (1985). MMPI scales for the DSM-III personality disorders: Their derivation and correlates. *Journal of Personality, 49,* 245-251.